AF248910

THEATER OF THE MIND

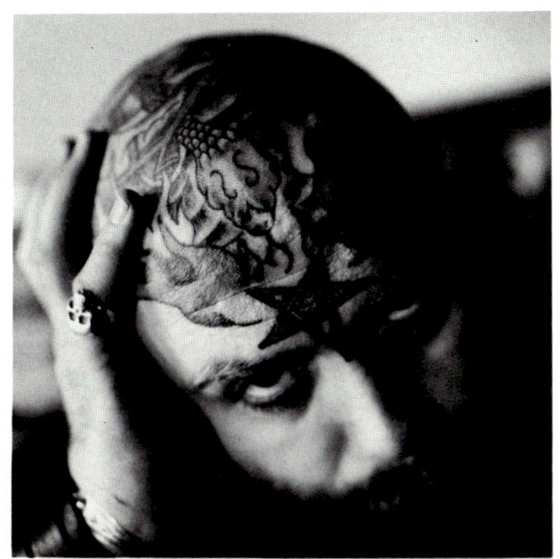

ARTHUR TRESS

MORGAN & MORGAN

1976

Morgan & Morgan, Inc.,
Publishers
145 Palisade Street
Dobbs Ferry, New York 10522

International Standard Book
Number 0-87100-106-3
Library of Congress Catalog
Card Number 76-25392

Printed in Quadradot Lithography
by Morgan Press, Incorporated

Cover photo: Balkin, tattoo by Spider Webb

Book design by David Laufer

The preparation of this book has been
partially funded by a grant from the
New York State Council on the Arts.

A limited edition portfolio of twelve prints
is available from the publisher.

PRELUDES

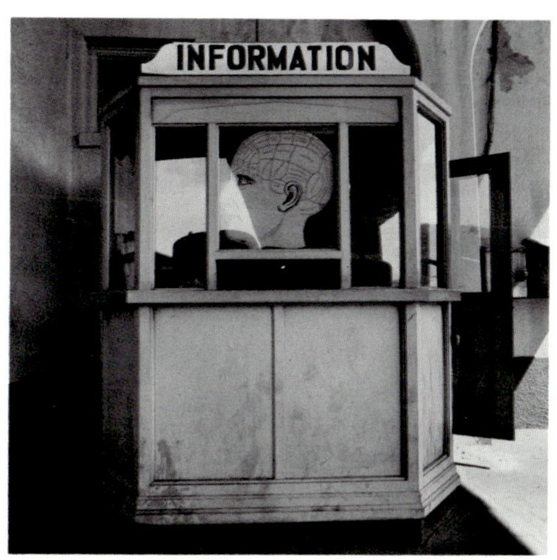

TRESS' VAUDEVILLE
by Duane Michals

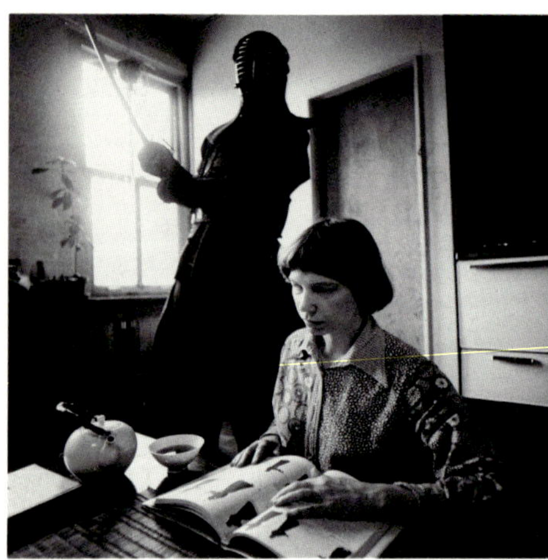

If Arthur Tress comes to photograph you, beware. Do not be taken in by that innocent smile and shy demeanor. They are his disguises. Arthur sees rather than looks, and he will see your secrets. I don't know quite how he does it. Tress will not just photograph your chin or nose or eyebrows. He will not seat you in front of a piece of white no-seam paper and pretend that a photograph of your wrinkles and a receding hairline is anything more than wrinkles and a receding hairline. And that bored look on your face is certainly a picture of boredom, not revelation or character. Actually that type of portrait has always been more insult than insight in my opinion. He has not been mesmerized by the camera's wonderful ability to describe and does not perpetuate the photographic myth that people are what they appear to be in front of a camera. Tress takes enormous chances and makes new demands on traditional ideas of what a photographic portrait might be, always a risky business. But he is up to that risk, and in expanding his photographic vocabulary, he also expands ours.

Tress will upset you. When he photographs you with a friend or lover, you will become an actor. You will perform in his theater and that drama one soon realizes is one's own. Don't be surprised if Arthur suddenly asks you to put your mother in a wheelbarrow, and don't be amazed to find yourself doing it. It all seems a joke, but when our smiles fade we are quietly shocked by what we are experiencing. Something disconcerting has happened. Looking at some of these photographs is like listening in on some strange family's argument. We are embarrassed and want to leave quietly, but don't. Ultimately the joke has been on us. What at first glance seemed corny and obvious now has become quite serious and makes us feel uncomfortable. And we are not used to this discomfort. Most photographers make us so comfortable that we fall asleep. We prefer photographers not to make demands on us.

Arthur is not nice. He irritates the way children do that ask too many questions. We wish that they would be quiet because we do not know the answers to those questions. Arthur does. It's not that he photographs all those things that are so readily seen between people. Rather that he intuits all those unseen ties of a relationship and brings them to our attention. Now we understand and nothing more needs to be said. It is a kind of photographic vaudeville, funny and sad.

I don't think that I want Arthur to photograph me. I might not be prepared to deal with what he sees. And I know he will be right.

ARTHUR TRESS
by Michel Tournier
of the Academie Goncourt, France.

Translated from L'Oeil by Evelyne Jesenof

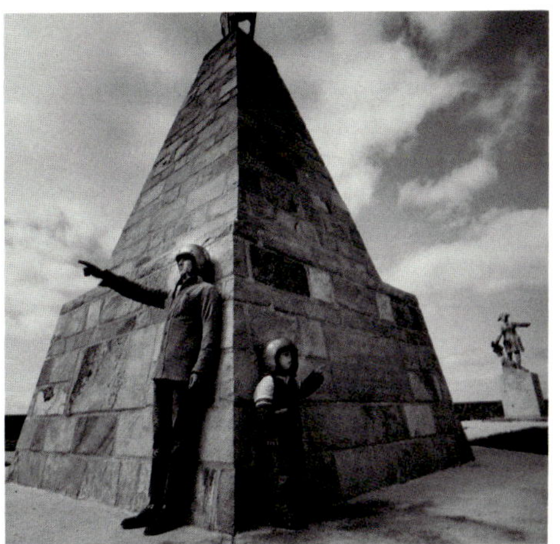

I would like to be able to say that I discovered Arthur Tress. But after further thought, he could more justifiably claim that he discovered me.

It all began approximately two years ago, just a short time after the publication of my book *The Ogre* in the United States. I received a letter from this unknown person. "Having read your book," he said, "I think that you will like my photographs." Following that came a package of photographs. I was shocked, dazzled and prodigiously interested.

At first impression and that goes a long way, I was struck by how in a series of pictures that flows from one inspirational source each image is so completely different. There is never any repetition and nowhere is there evidence of the stream drying up. While each photograph, itself a vein, is extinguished, it seems, by that single picture, the flow of genius is contained in the very next. At the same time all his works are inhabited by the same spirit, and they all deal with the same theme. Basically it's always the same but on the surface, the newness is always total and absolute. Each time we begin over again. That is the rarity of having a "vision."

What then is this unique theme that we find repeated in totally unexpected forms from image to image? Let us not delude ourselves into thinking that we will be able to define this in a definitive and exhaustive fashion. We won't be able to do it simply because Arthur Tress is a true creator. One imprisons a formula, a recipe, an ideology, an idea only by the gush of creation. Paul Valery: "If the esthetic could be, a work of art would necessarily disappear when put

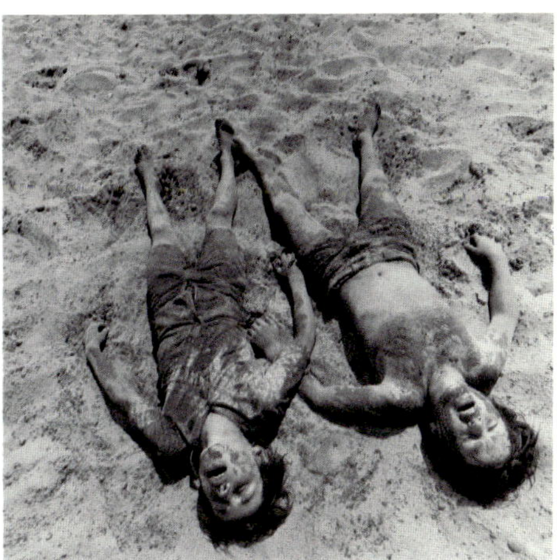

face to face with it the way it does when faced with its own essence." Therefore because esthetic cannot be, let's attempt several approaches—five approaches—to the mystery of Arthur Tress of the 1000 faces.

Oppression The anguish of being the prisoner of a mass. A web of strings or ribbons, a funnel, a mask, an envelope made of some sort of plastic material, a jar of pickles, a garbage can, a sewer hole, an elevator, a water main. The anguish of being crushed by a ball, a mechanical horse, etc.

These are classic nightmare themes, but Arthur Tress' art consists in giving them tremendous credibility by placing them in a

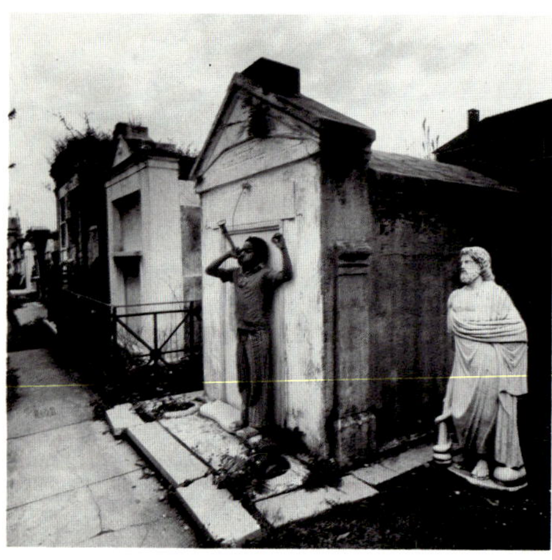

totally realistic context. He does not allow for the enchantment part of the nightmare which normally allows it to be tolerable.

His images force us to believe what they are relating to us. It can be added that he is greatly aided by the environment that the United States puts at his disposal. One can hardly imagine these images in Europe. But does one ever know for sure with this devil of a man?

Death Its cadaverous profile overshadows more than one of these stage productions. There is even within Arthur Tress an ascent towards necrophilia: let him follow it but ascend it! The cadaver is passivity and therefore its obscenity is formidably seductive.

The Child Is the privileged witness. Witness: One who sees, who knows, who remembers. But also: object of proof, undergoing tests, corpus delicti. Of all the corpus delicti, the body of a child is the most charming. The child is the privileged object of sadism and necrophilia. But he is also hope, because perhaps tomorrow, having become strong, he will take revenge.

Liberation In more than one work by Arthur Tress, beyond the oppression, the horizon opens, a gaping door, a staircase flying upwards toward the sky. This freeing is not accessible to the oppressed. Yet it is there, it haunts him, it is promised.

Complicity Photographers generally have a fundamental idea of reality. Things and people are presented in their naive spontaneity. The "contrivance" is a terrible sin that he conceals as best he can, that he denies madly.

Arthur Tress worries about "ethics" as though it was bad luck. He makes fire from all wood with perfect tranquility of the soul, taking from stores, museums and theatre props—or simply from his pockets which hold all the accessories that his photography needs, from the stuffed rat to the Tyrolienne pipe as well as the monstrance, the halbert or the hernia belt. With anyone else a similar off-handedness would lead to the breaking down of the image. We would laugh or shrug our shoulders. Here it works. Everything works. Arthur Tress always unites the conditions of a general complicity. That of the people being photographed, that of the objects, that of the landscapes, and ours, on top of everything else!

I met Arthur Tress long after I had lived with his pictures. I was a little frightened. I imagined a rough and boorish man, perhaps even a little dirty, to whom one must indulge everything for the sake of his genius. Instead I saw arrive a young man who was frail and timid, worried on every side, concealing a wounded look behind a theological student's glasses. But inside his photographer's bag was a medallion with a portrait of Franz Kafka. There without doubt is the most apparent clue to the Tress mystery.

INTRODUCTION
by A. D. Coleman

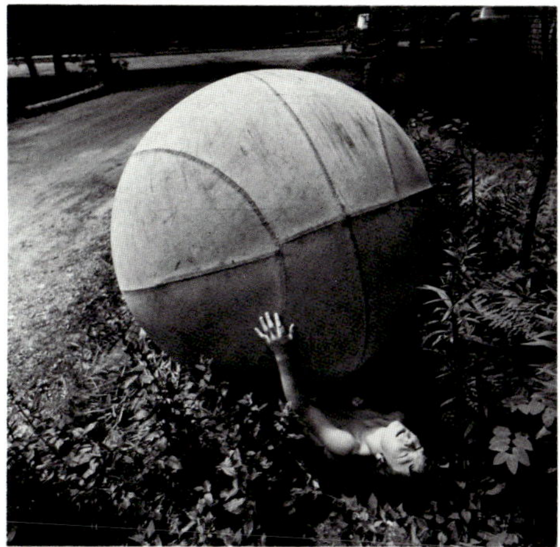

All photographs are fictions, to a far greater extent than we are yet able or willing to acknowledge. Yet most of them still pretend to a high degree of verisimilitude and transparency, to the impersonal neutrality of windows on the world.

It is in the directorial mode of photography more than any other that the fictional nature of the photographic image is not only recognized and explored but openly declared as an active premise, a hermeneutical stance. This mode might most simply be defined as the deliberate staging of events for the express purpose of making photographs thereof — as distinguished from addressing oneself through the camera to an ongoing, uncontrolled, external "reality."

Though you wouldn't know it from studying any of the available histories of the medium, the directorial mode of photography has a long, diverse, and honorable tradition. Yet for reasons which appear to have more to do with photo-historical politics than with scholarship and logic, certain uses (and users) of the directorial mode have been accepted as legitimate while others have been rejected out of hand. The basis for these usually arbitrary judgements generally boils down to the conservative taste patterns of the medium's heretofore dominant historians.

Thus it has been considered aesthetically permissible for the late Paul Strand to "cast" his book on an Italian village, *Un Paese,* by having the townspeople lined up and selecting from them those he considered most picturesque — but unacceptable for Edward Curtis to persuade American Indians to reenact rituals and events out of their past; valid for Edward Weston to ar-

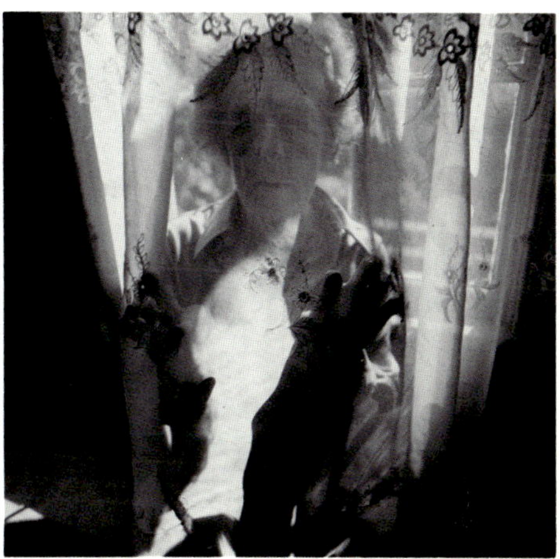

range vegetables and nudes in static, preconceived configurations in his studio — but not for William Mortensen to use his studio as the setting for those mini-dramas which were the basis of his stylized, Symbolist allegories.

Fortunately, a generation of photographers has come of age whose members are intent on overriding this and all other prejudices concerning the "proper" uses of their medium. One result of their refusal to be trapped within these whimsical boundaries has been the resurgence of work in the directorial mode. A list of the most influential and prolific contemporary workers

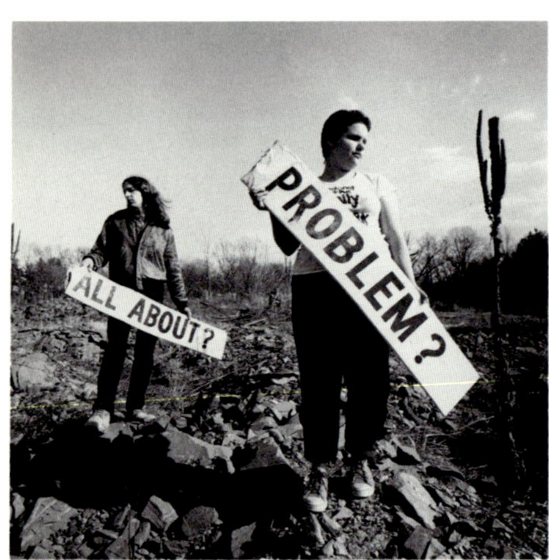

in this form would have to include Leslie Krims, Ralph Eugene Meatyard, Richard Kirstel, Lucas Samaras, Clarence John Laughlin, Duane Michals, Eikoh Hosoe — and Arthur Tress.

An essentially theatrical attitude has been a hallmark of Arthur Tress' imagery since his public debut as a photographer.

The first themes he addressed were nominally topical ones: pollution, ecology, and the claustrophobia of life in urban sinks. One of Tress' primary concerns has always been the various ways in which the world (the physical world, in this case) impinges upon the individual's sense of freedom and psychic territory. Tress photographed his understandings of the causes and effects of these problems, and their possible solutions, in several fashions. Though sometimes his observations were presented in conventional photographic terms, as often as not he found ways and means (through the use of volunteer actors, props, and other devices) to dramatize those conditions and situations which he found to be most significant.

This penchant for photographic *tableaux vivants* became even more pronounced in his next extended work, a series of photographs depicting the fantasies and dreams of children. Almost without exception, these were carefully staged productions of specific scenarios which had been recounted by children to the photographer. Tress scouted appropriate locations, provided the necessary costumes and props, and photographed the children themselves acting out their own inner visions. The photograph became the proscenium arch; the viewer became the audience.

This suite was followed, several years later, by a "novel in photographs" whose protagonist was Tress himself, portrayed through his own shadow in an extended sequence of ingenious and intelligent images, all set up and acted out. *Shadow* is an ambitious experiment in photographic storytelling, reminiscent on several levels of the wordless woodblock-print novels of Lynd Ward. Like many of Ward's books, this one is also an account of a picaresque spiritual voyage; in Tress' work the adventurer travels through space and time in a symbolic, allegorical, and (one presumes) autobiographical narrative.

The evolution of Tress' imagery, then, has been towards an increasingly directorial approach and increasingly personal themes. If *The Dream Collector* is (albeit by proxy) an expression of the photographer's own childhood traumas, and *Shadow* the tale of

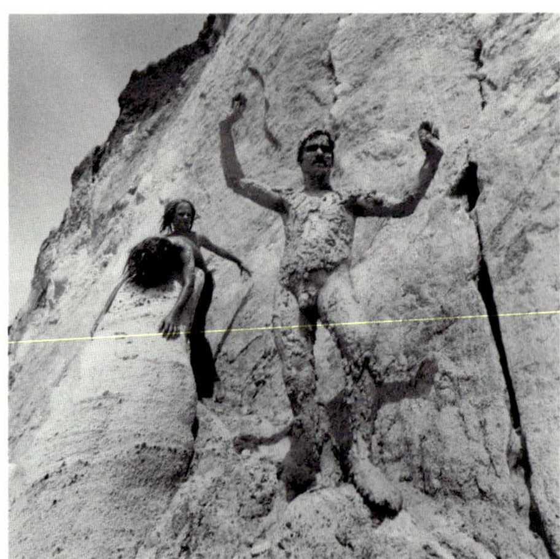

his coming of age, then this new book is about him in the here and now, a catalogue of his own ongoing concerns and obsessions.

It is obviously not coincidental that the photographer's background includes the study of film directing techniques and Kabuki theatre; the impact of these disciplines on his work is apparent. Similarly, it should come as no great surprise to learn that his interests include psychology, ethnography, eastern philosophy, magic and the supernatural; his imagery is consistently attuned to the manifestations of power in personal and cultural mythology, and the harmonies and discords between the two.

The areas that he probes in this book reflect those predilections. All these photographs are about human beings enmeshed in what Carlos Castaneda would call their own "separate realities." Sometimes the universes in which they operate are no larger than a nuclear family; sometimes they are as infinite as the reach of necromancy.

Is it accidental that we speak of "darkroom magic?" Or that the camera is often suspected—even by comparative sophisticates—of stealing souls? Or that Arthur Tress collects boxes full of images of himself and other people living out their fantasies? I think not. A photographer in touch with him/herself makes photographs about what is essential in his/her experience. For Arthur Tress this involves the premeditated creation of images symbolizing the darker side of human nature. It is paradoxical and somewhat unnerving that he does so in a peculiarly forthright and even cheerful way, but that seems always to have been an aspect of his style.

Regardless of subject, his images are clear, precise, articulate, intelligent. Because they are intended to communicate fairly specific understandings—be they intellectual, emotional, or both—they are open, careful, and ordered. This accessibility and structural consideration are purposeful: they are intended to entice you in and soothe your reason sufficiently so that the images can play freely in the non-linear, non-explanatory areas of the mind. At their best, the photographs of Arthur Tress are oddly enjoyable artifacts which provoke potentially volatile questions.

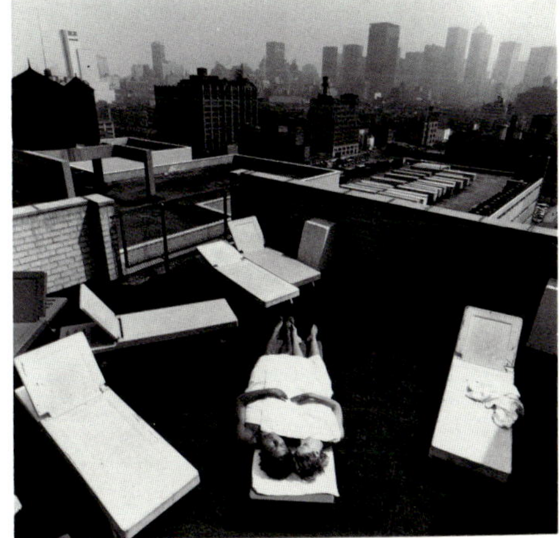

Thus we might look at any of these images and ask: What's going on here?

We are accustomed to looking at photographs of events as documents, slices of life excised (ideally) with such surgical precision and speed from the body of so-called "reality" that the flow of that reality is unaltered, the surgeon unobserved. But that is obviously not the case in this instance, since these particular events most likely would not have taken place were it not for the photographer's instigation of them and the participants' conscious cooperation. In that sense, therefore, these are ironic, false documents. Yet photographs, as we know (or at least think we know) are evidence; what, then, do these images demonstrate?

Well. They indicate that somewhere out there are people—quite a few of them, in fact—who are willing to act out very specific, often frightening, and rarely flattering self-portrayals and metaphors for their private experiences. What personal histories do they imply, and how do they connect with our own? These images also indicate that the participants are willing to perform their psychodramas in front of a camera, as active collaborators in the creation of images for others, even strangers, to see. What impels them to do so? Why, feeling as they must—because we all do in this culture—that the photograph is a credible facsimile of reality, are they desirous of making these otherwise secret realities of theirs visible and explicit? Under what set of psychic circumstances is each of us able to accept a camera in someone else's hands as a vehicle for our own self-expression, not just a mirror? What would it be like to live in a culture where it was an accepted practice to externalize all one's deepest feelings in images?

We might eventually be led to ask: Who are these people? And because these photographs make it apparent that there is someone interested in their ritualistic revelations, adept at evoking them from his subject and capable of embodying them in direct, effective, exorcistic images, another question follows: Who is this photographer?

CHILD'S PLAY

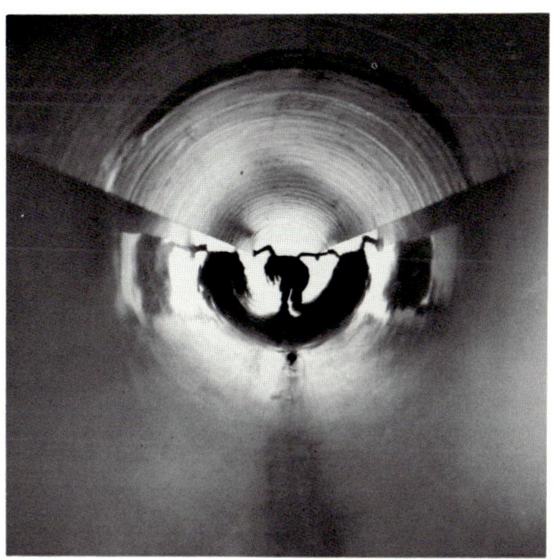

Boys on Castle, Atlantic City, New Jersey

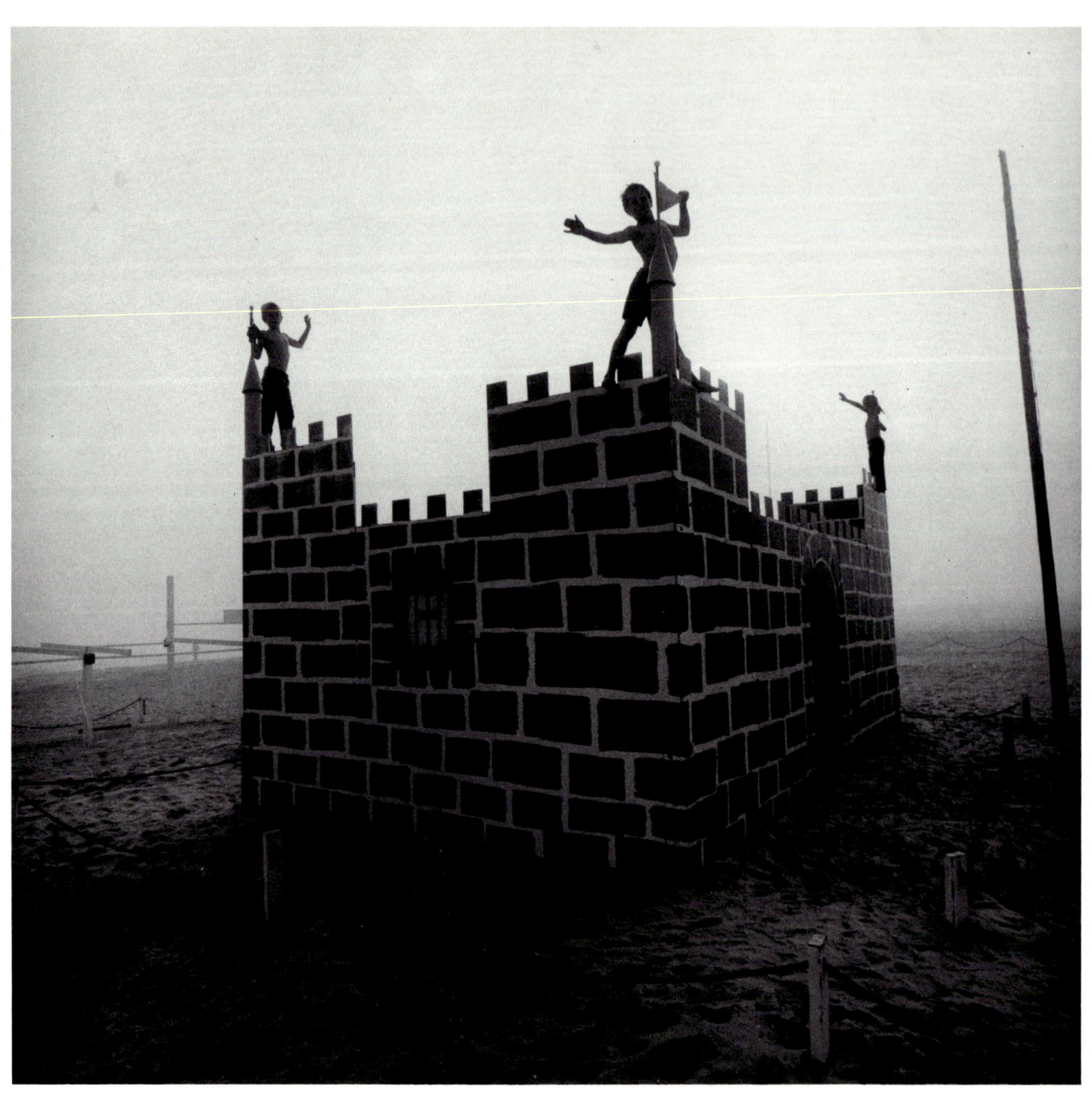

Boys on Checkerfloor, Far Rockaway, New York

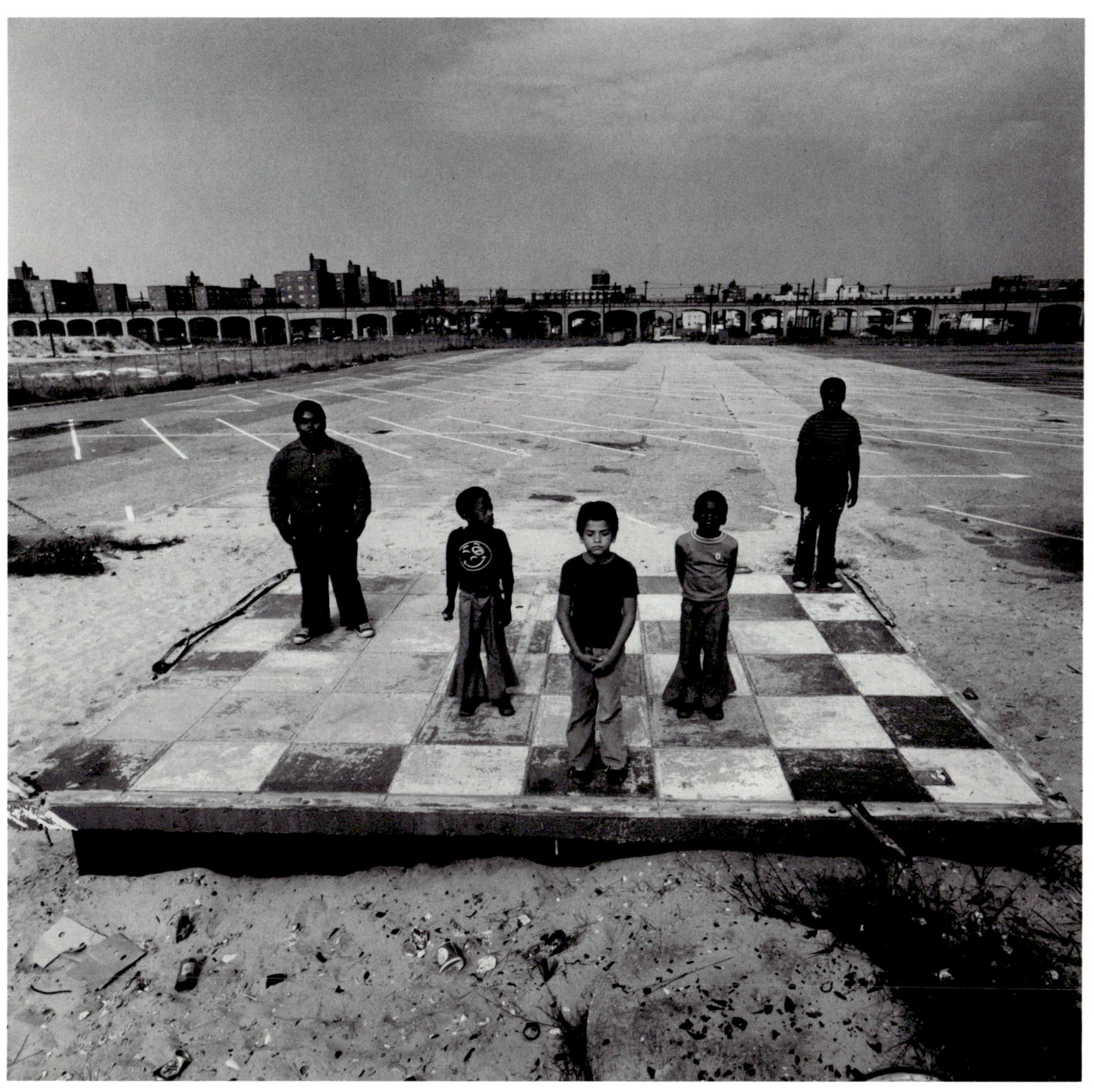

Girl with Mask, Rhinebeck, New York

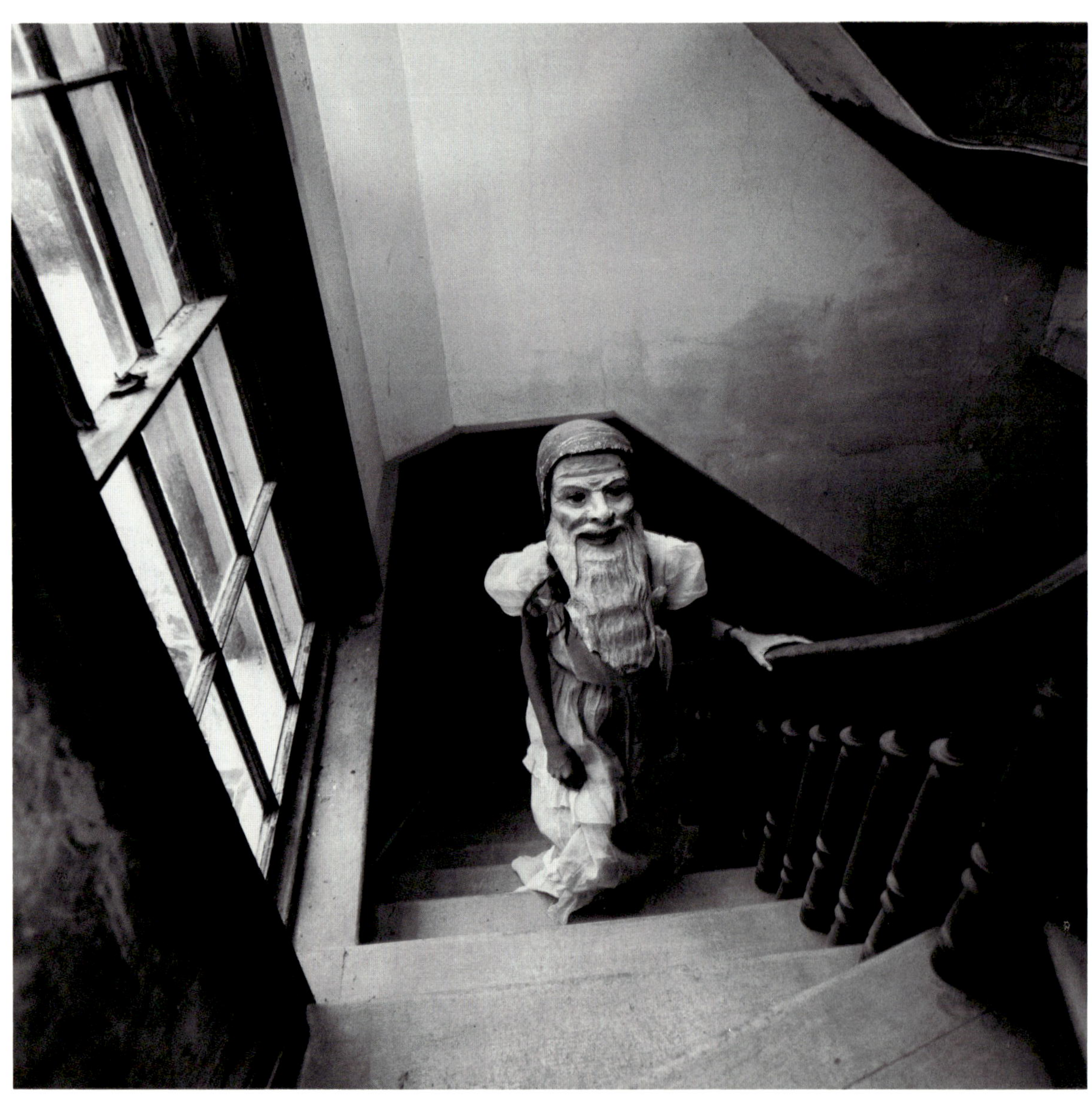

Boys with Road Guards, Coney Island, New York

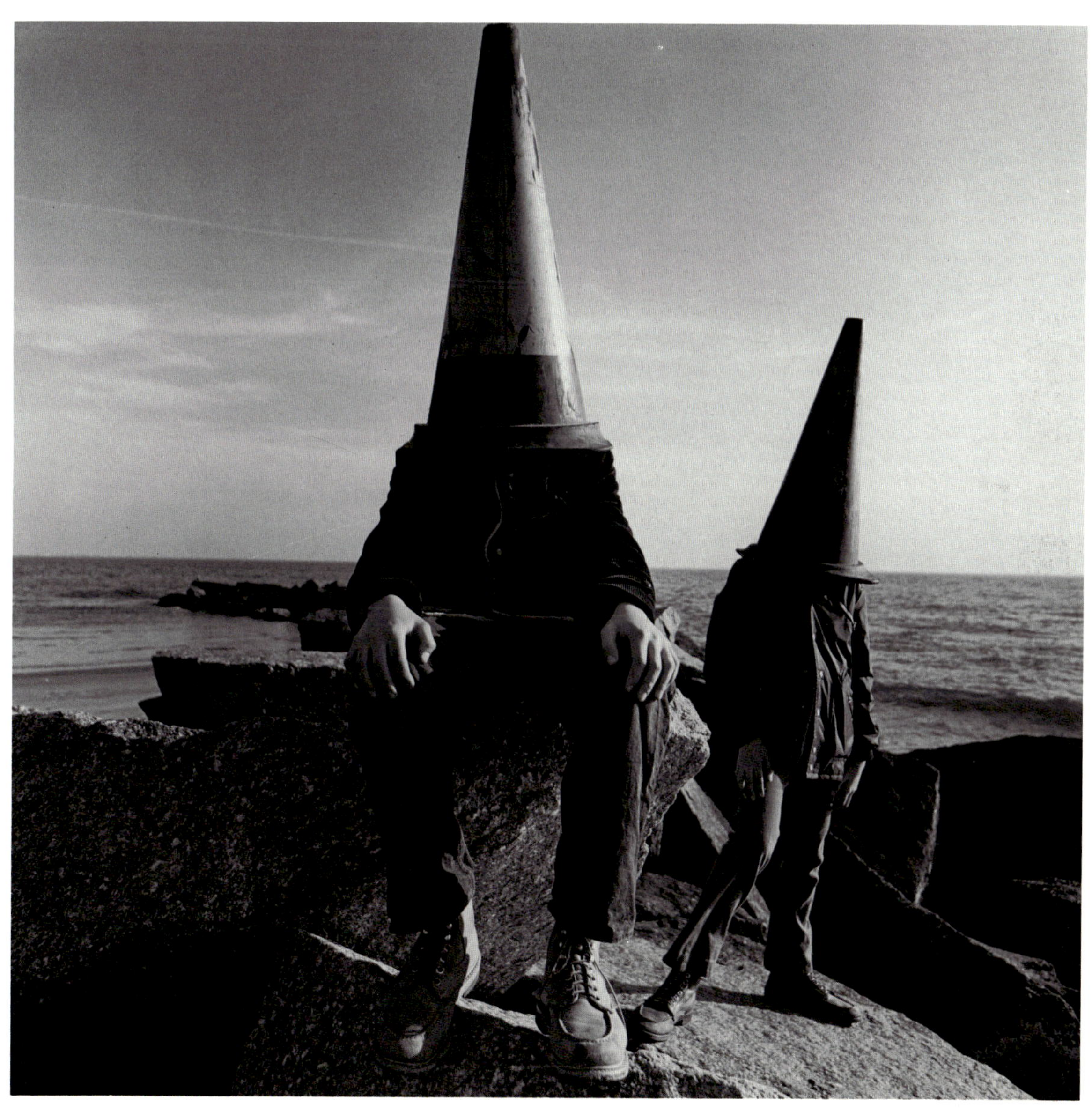

Boy in Flood Mud, Pittsburgh, Pennsylvania

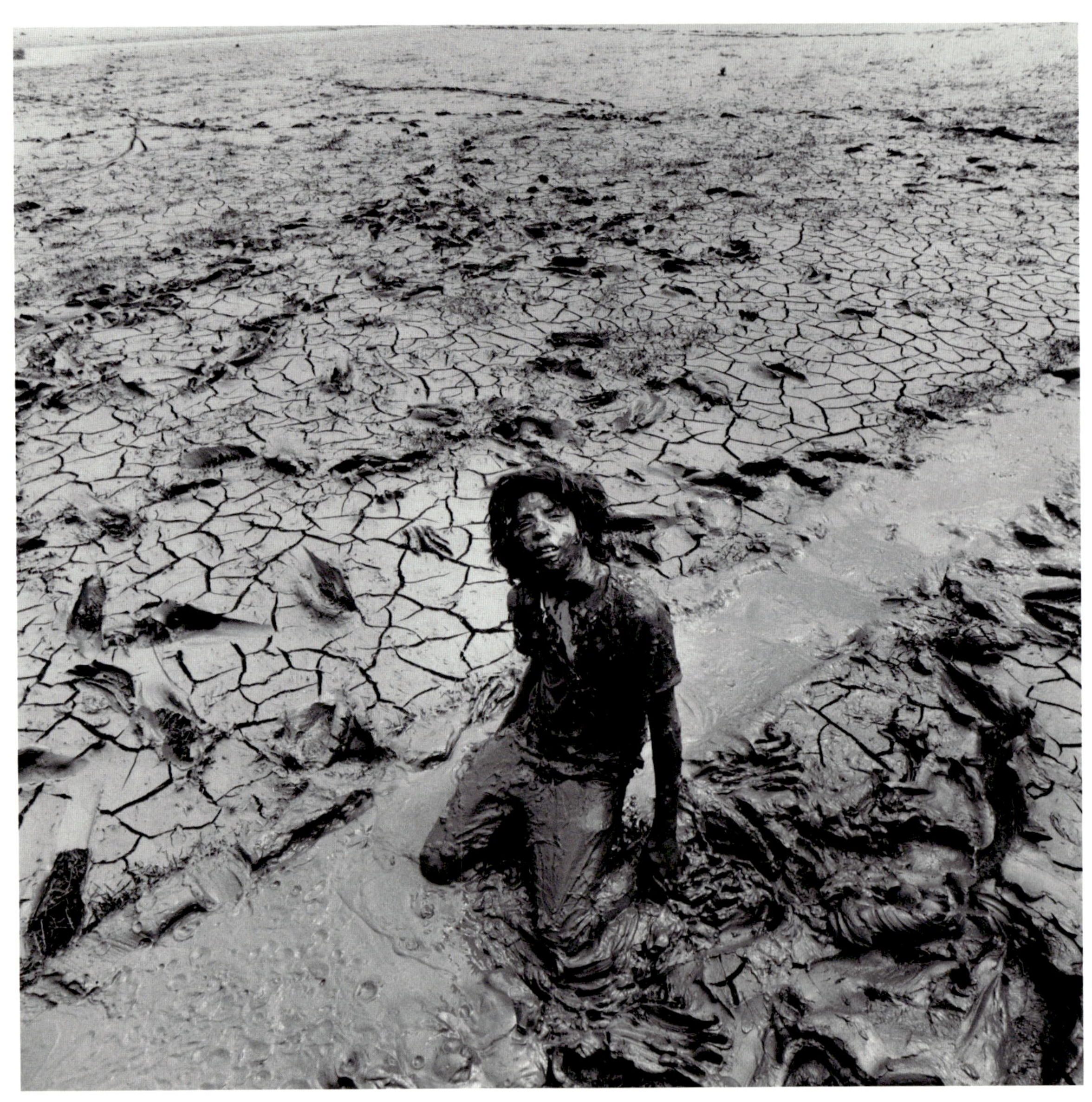

Boy in Stream, Caracas, Venezuela

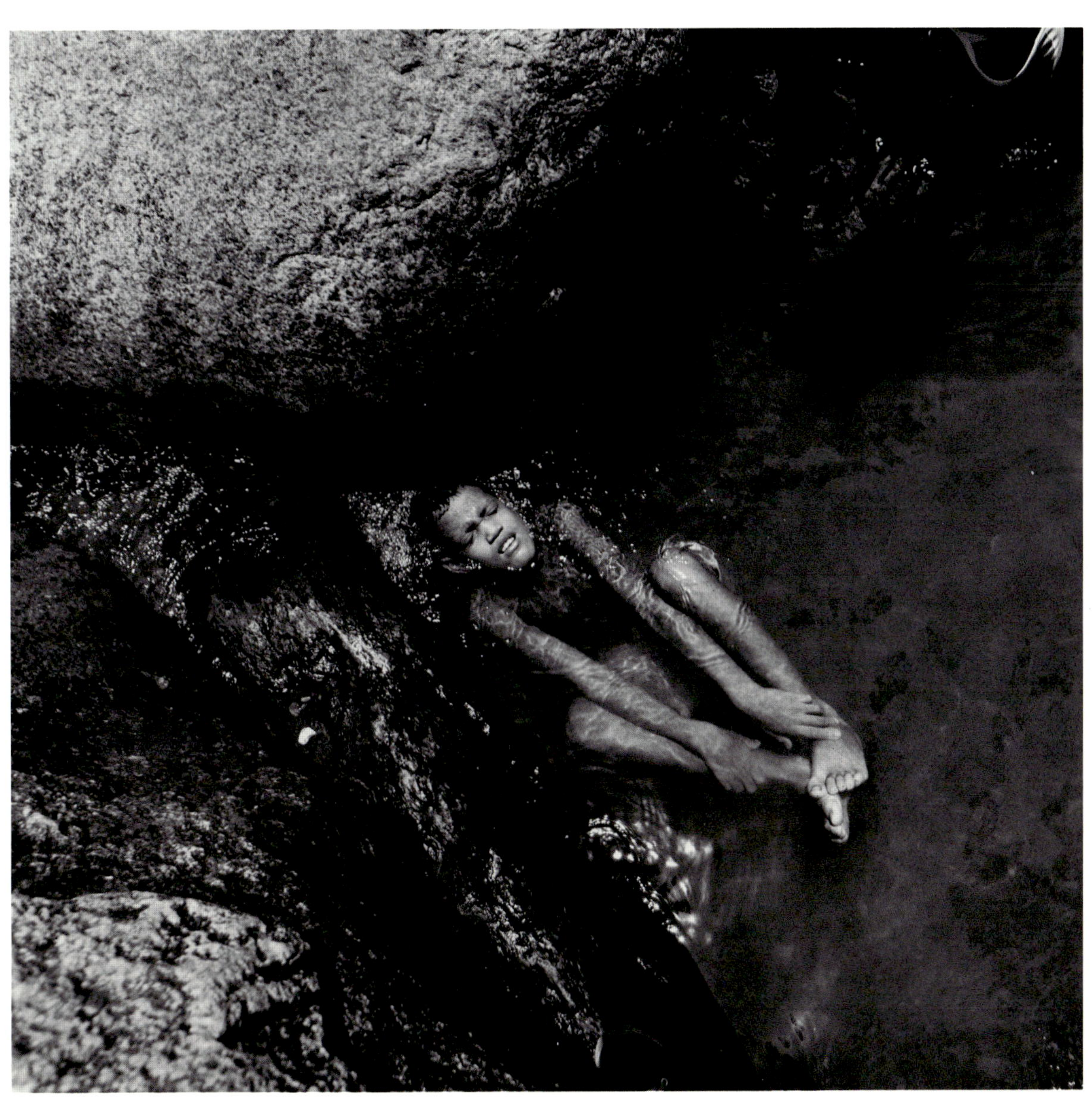

Boy and Cutout Face, Chinatown, New York

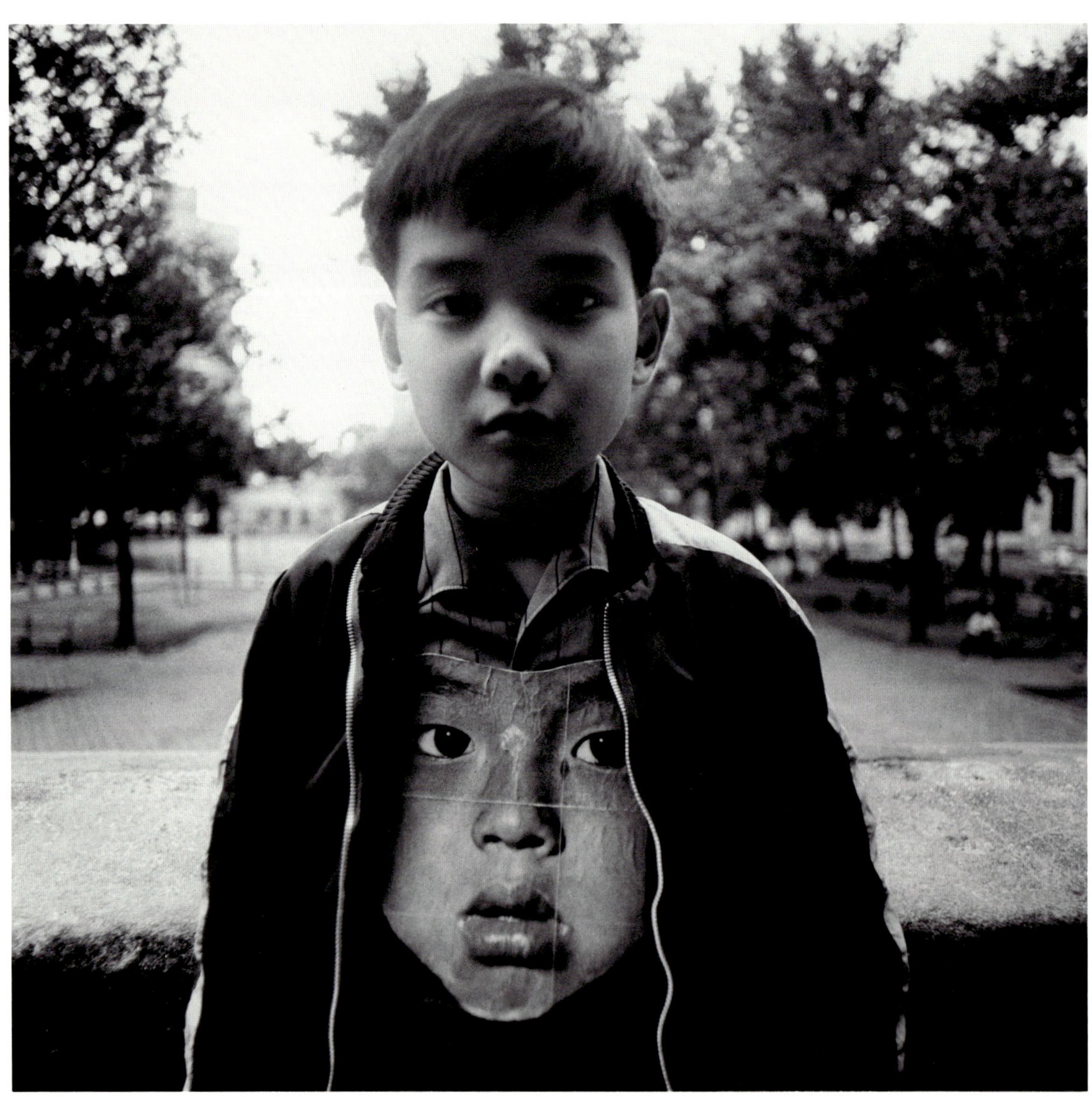

Hockey Player, New York City

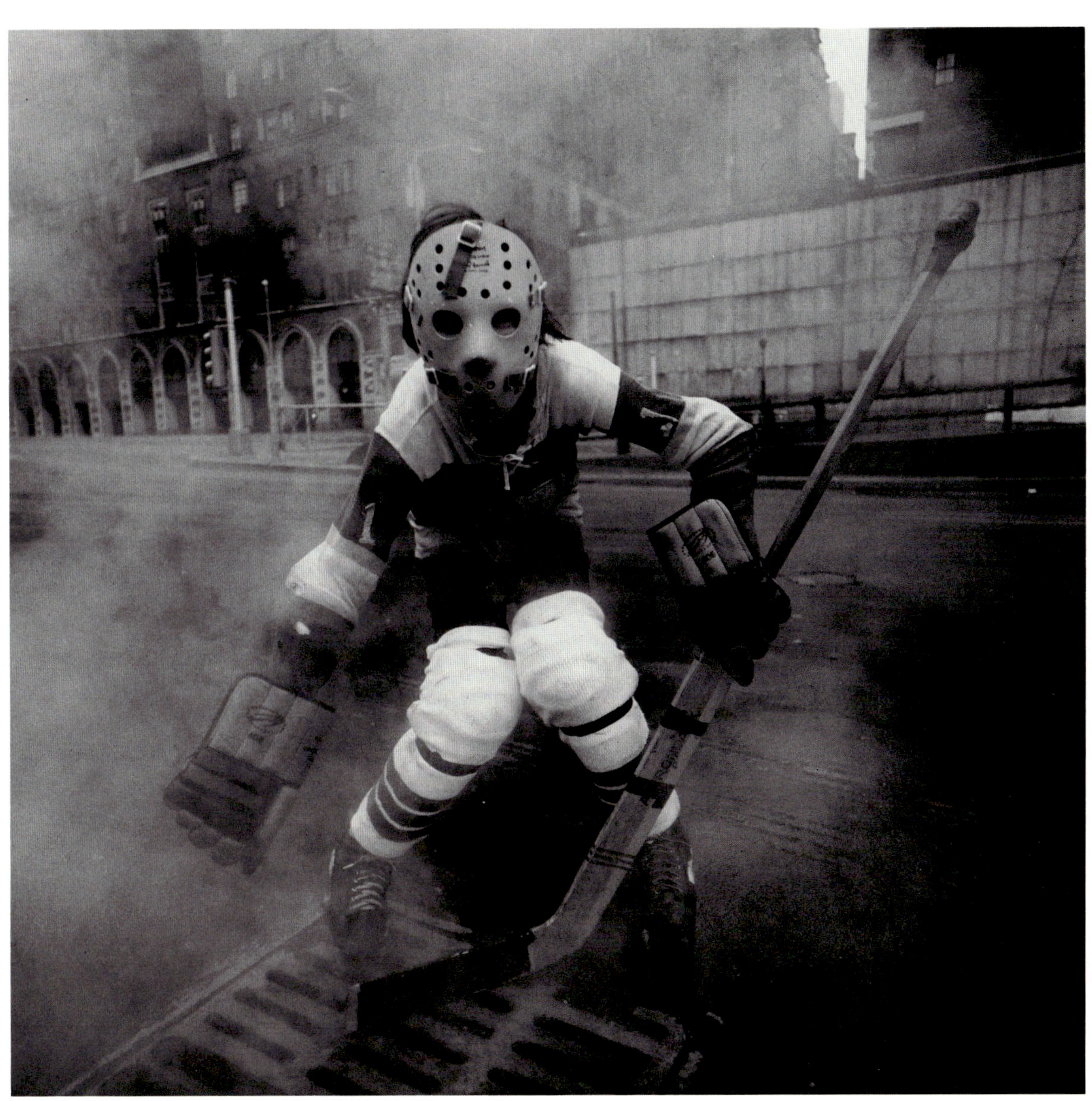

Girl with Sea Mammals, San Francisco, California

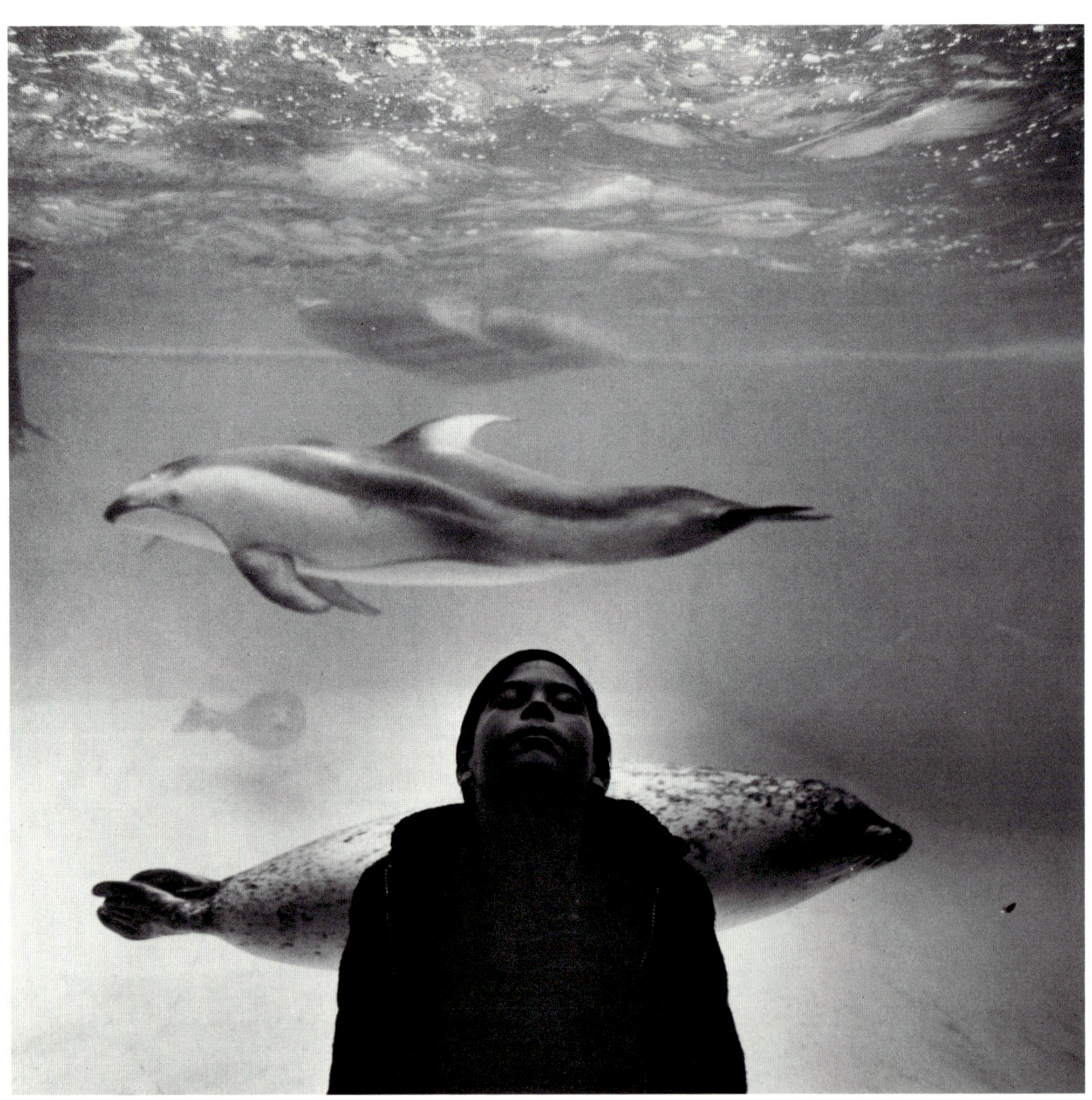

Boy on Wrecked Boat, Paradise Island, Bahamas

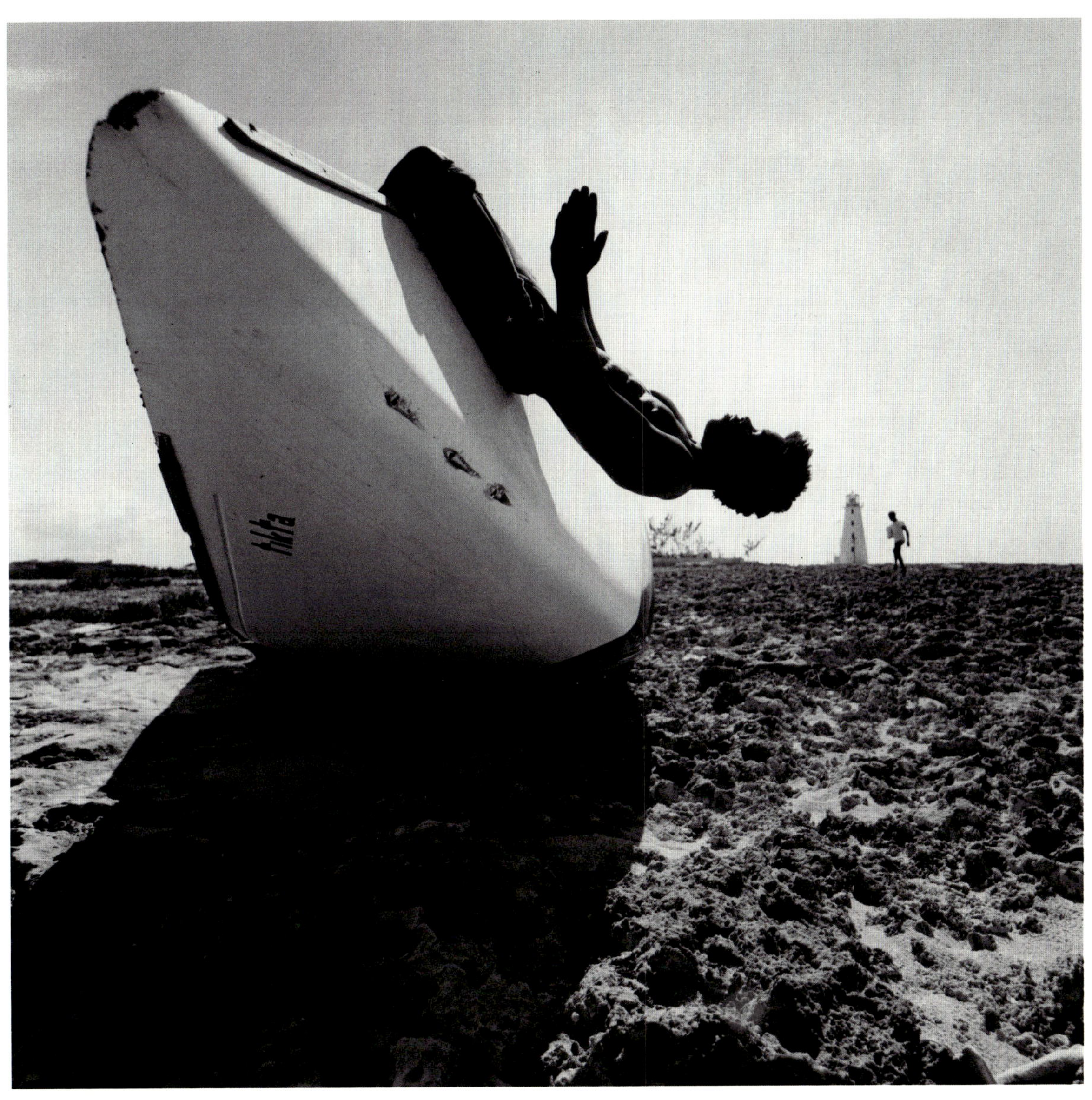

Girl and Carnival Statue, Coney Island, New York

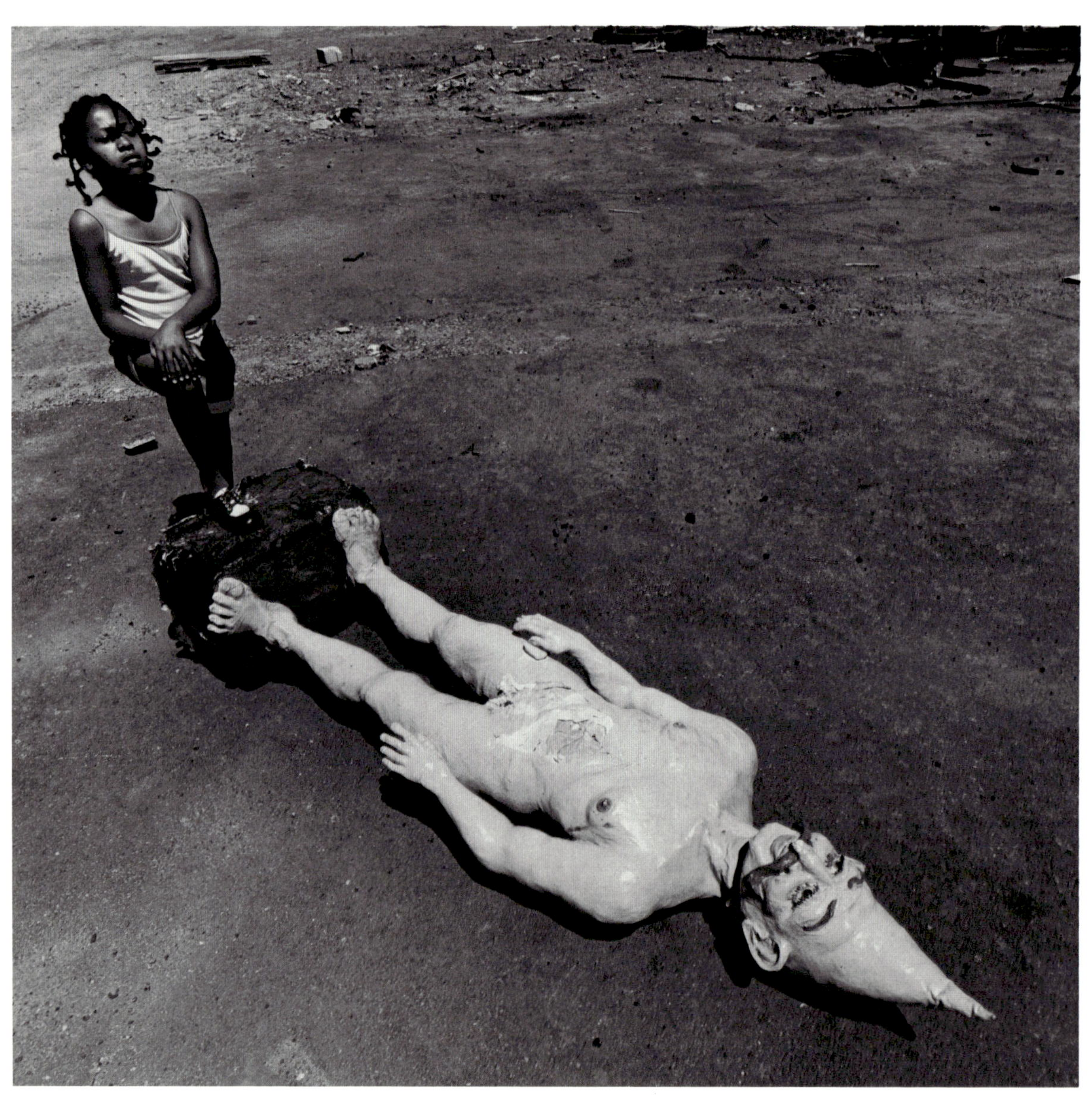

Girl with Eagle, Wood's Hole, Massachusetts

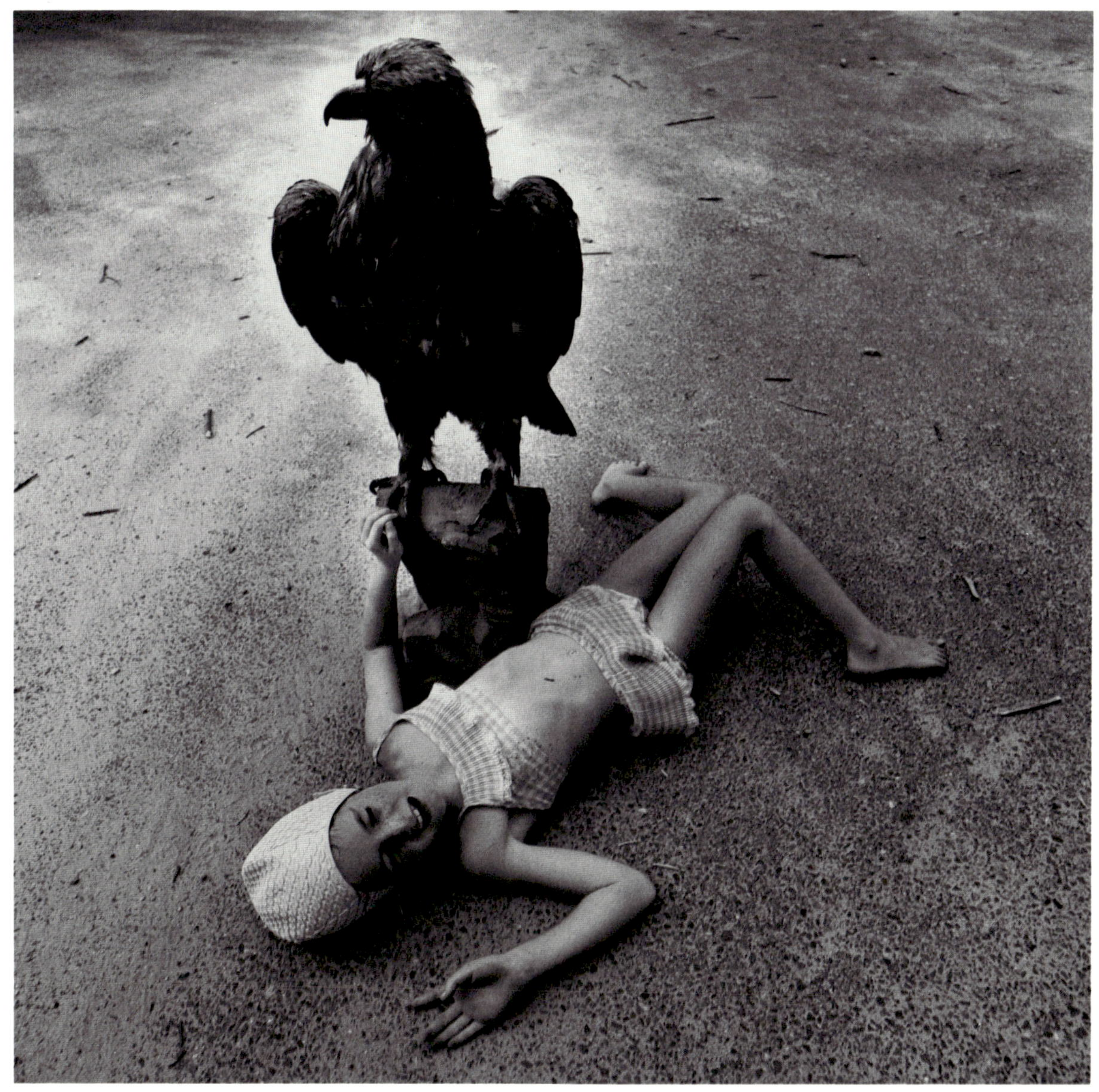

Anne under Window, Van Etten, New York

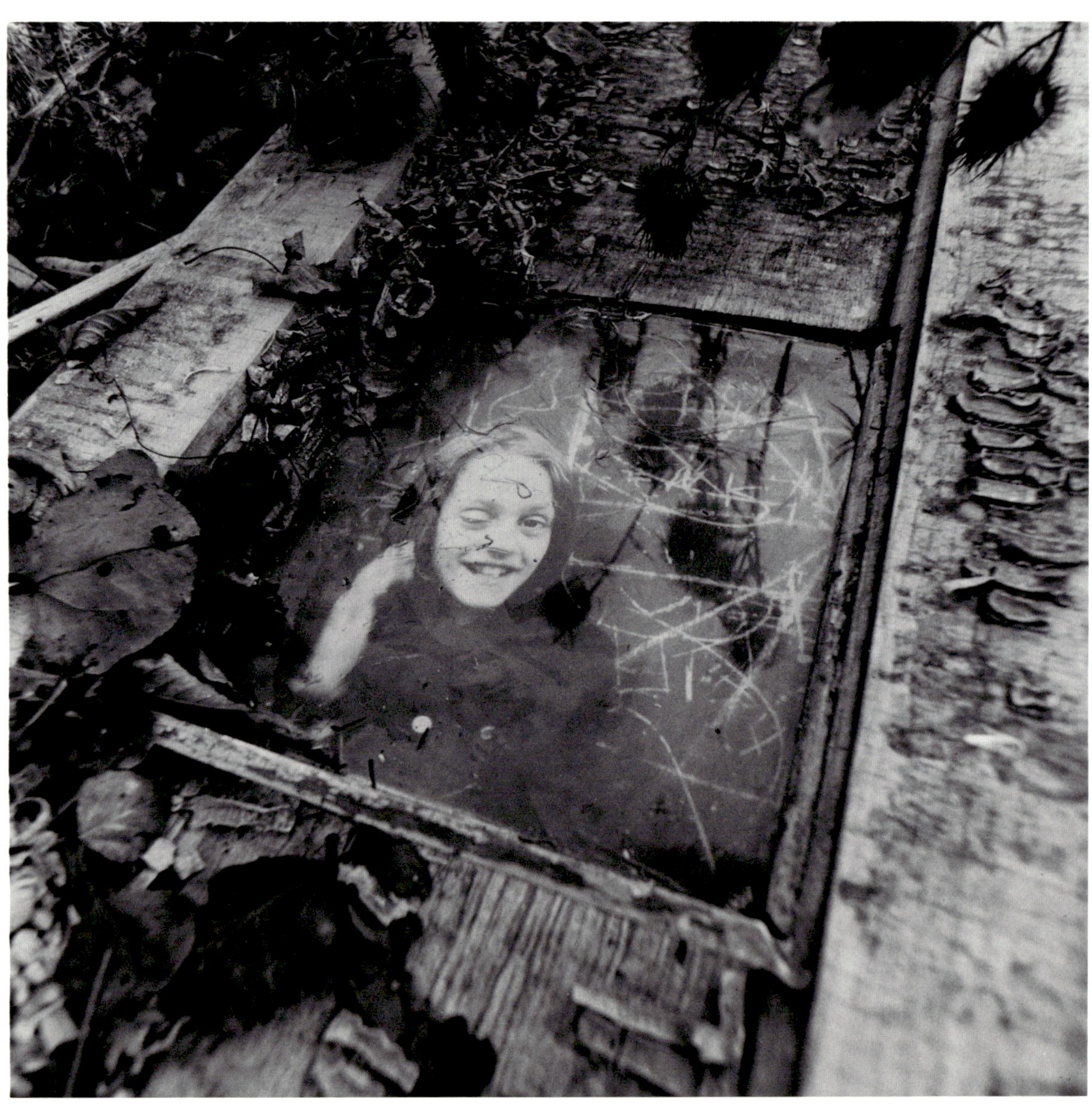

Susan and Burning Leaves, Riverside Drive Park, New York City

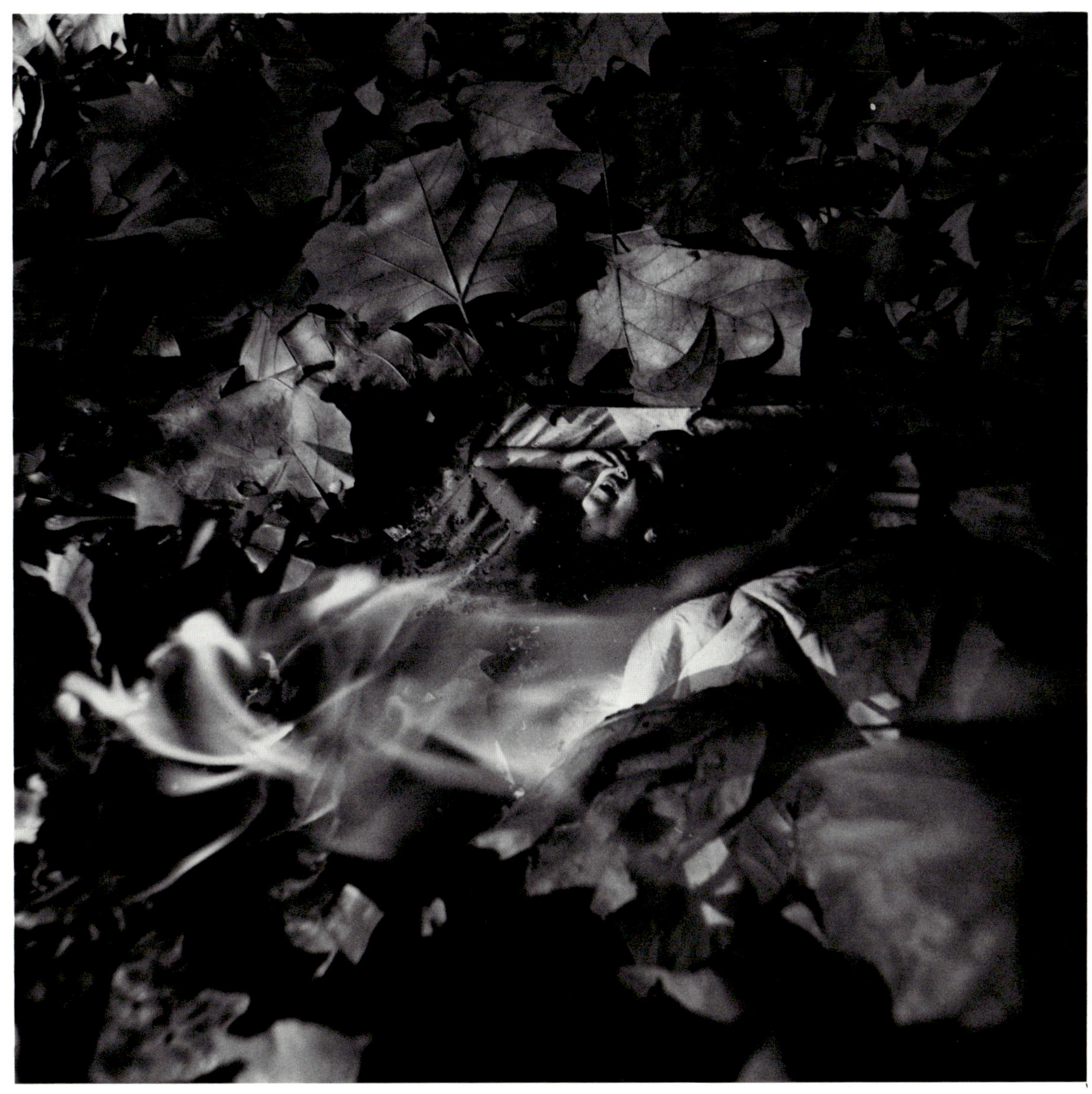

PRIVATE ACTS

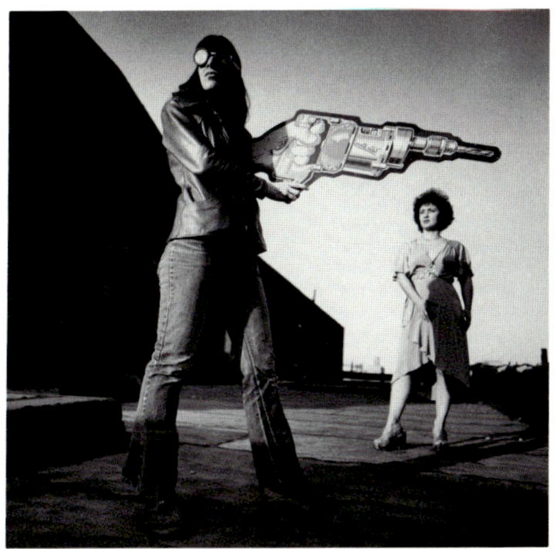

Ursule Molinaro and Peter St. Mu, New York City

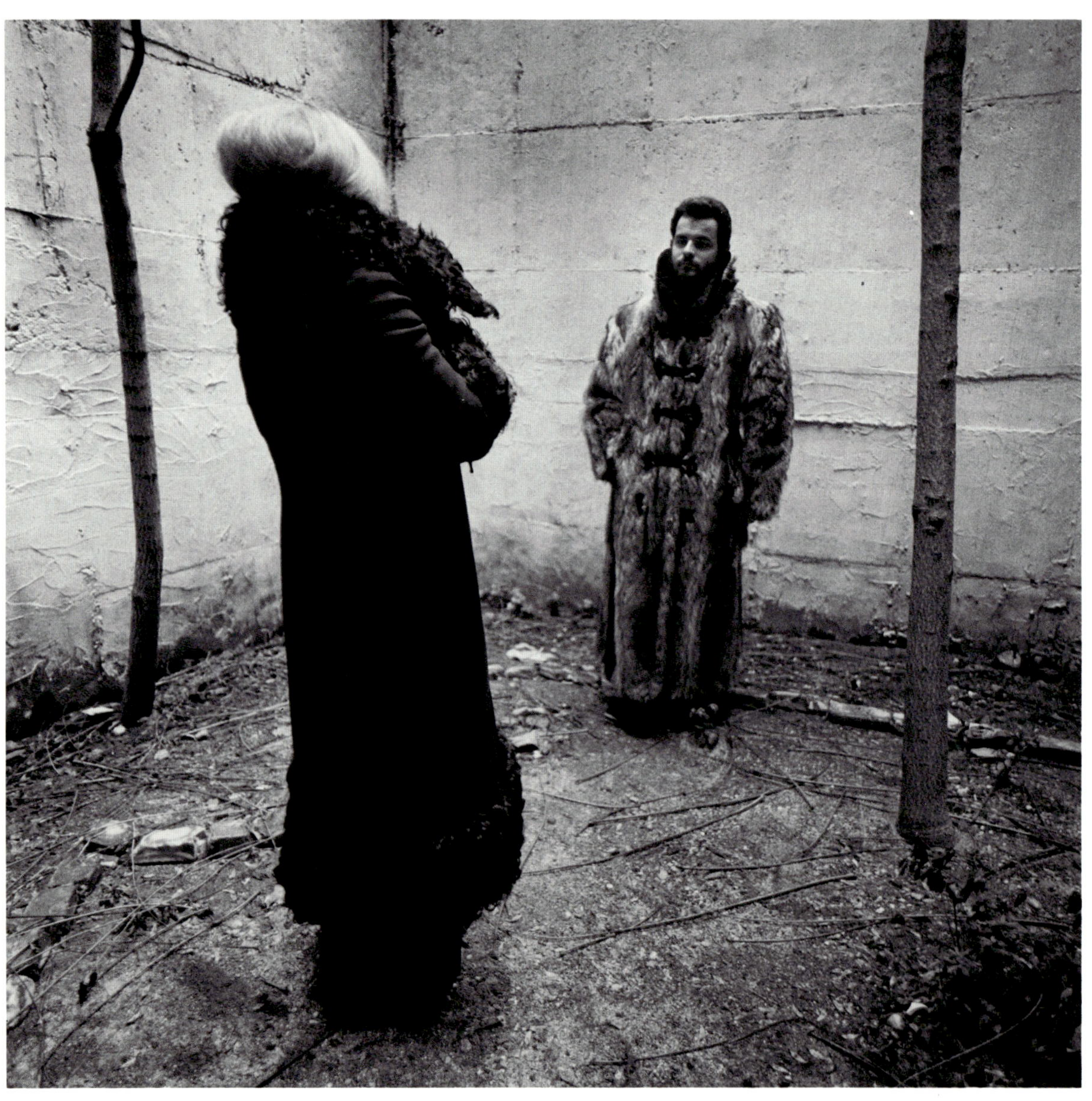

E. W. Towle and Michael, New York City

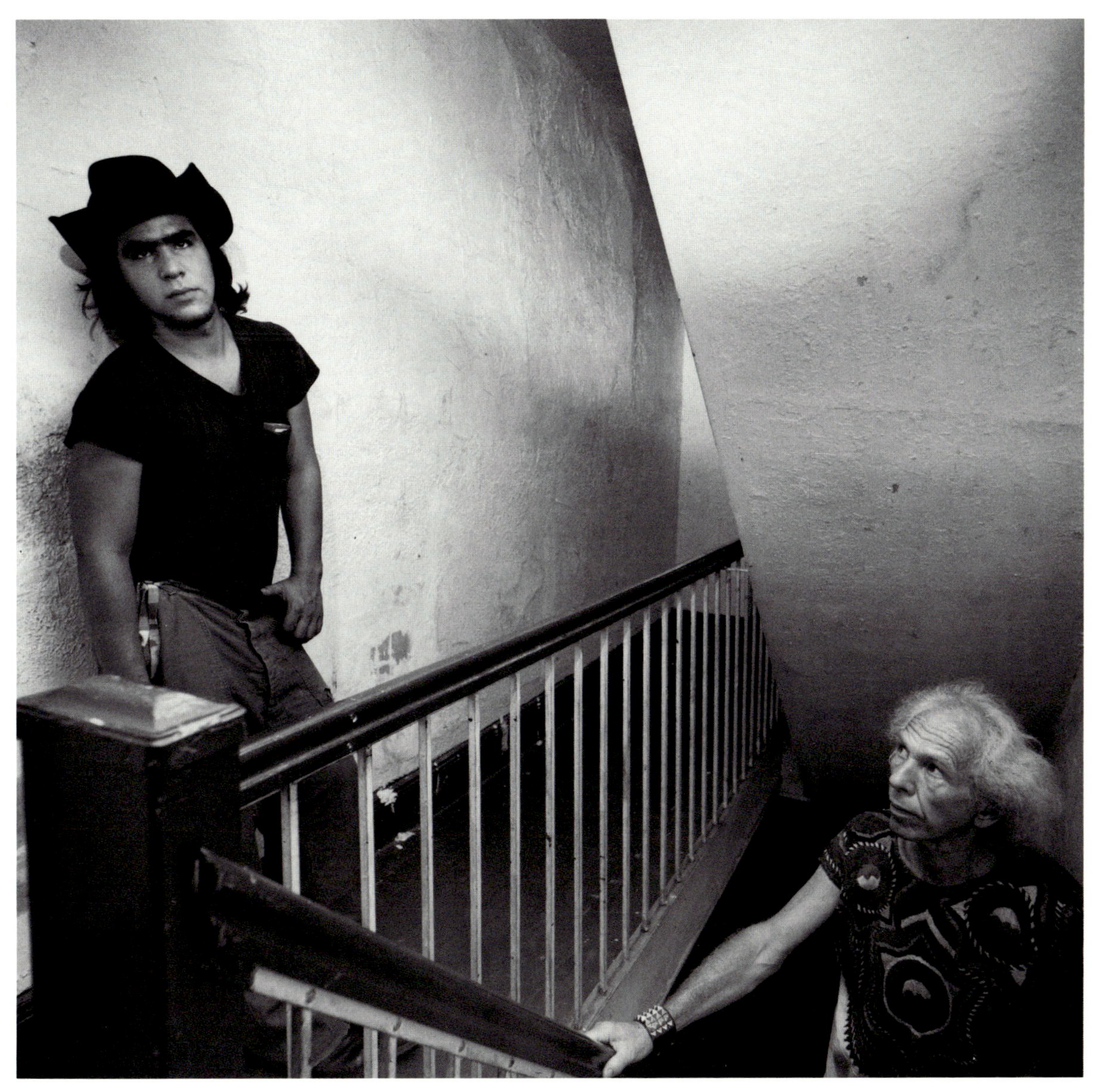

Girl collecting Goldfish, Chateau Breteuil, France

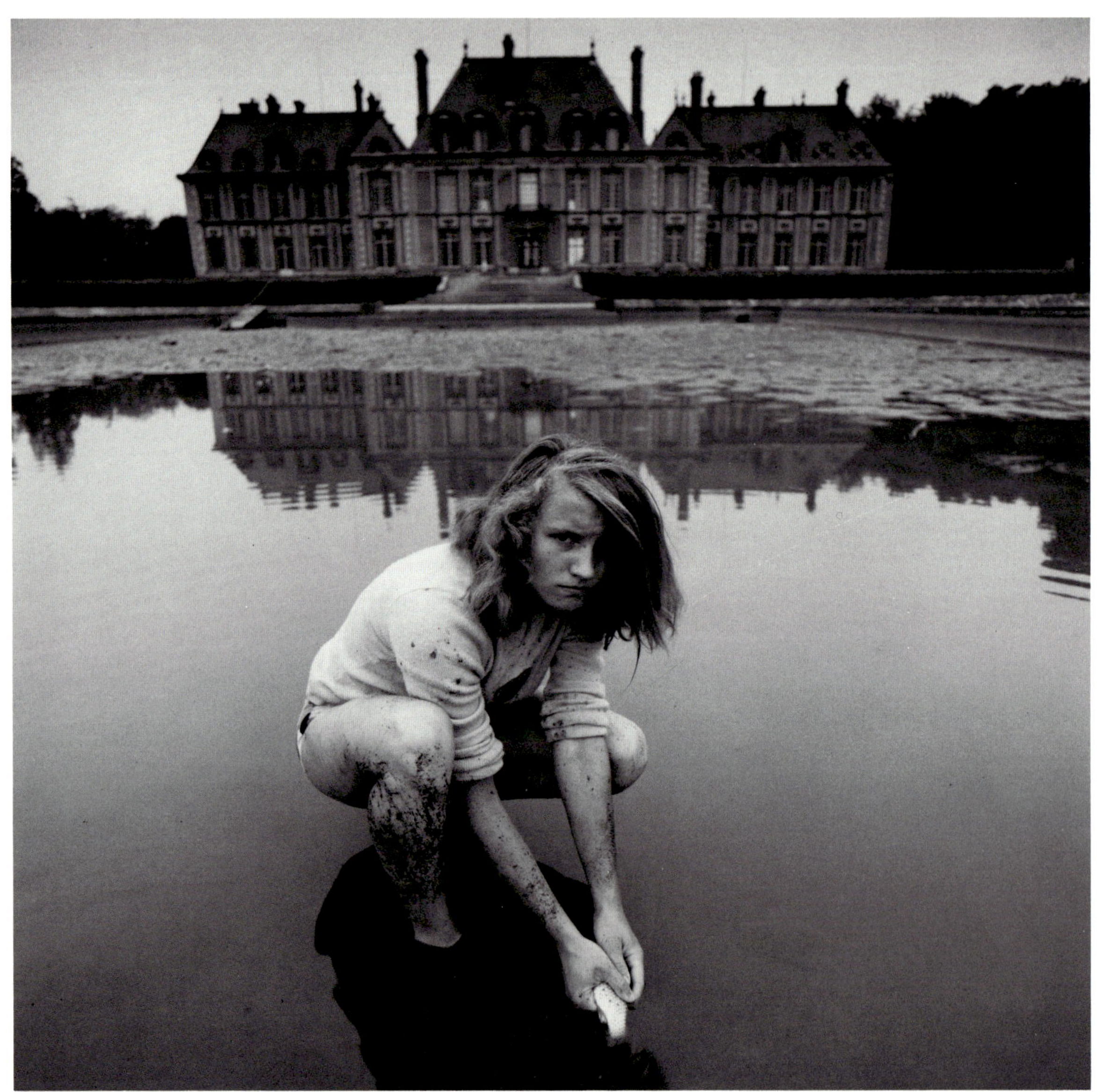

Bob Leet and Sheep, San Francisco, California

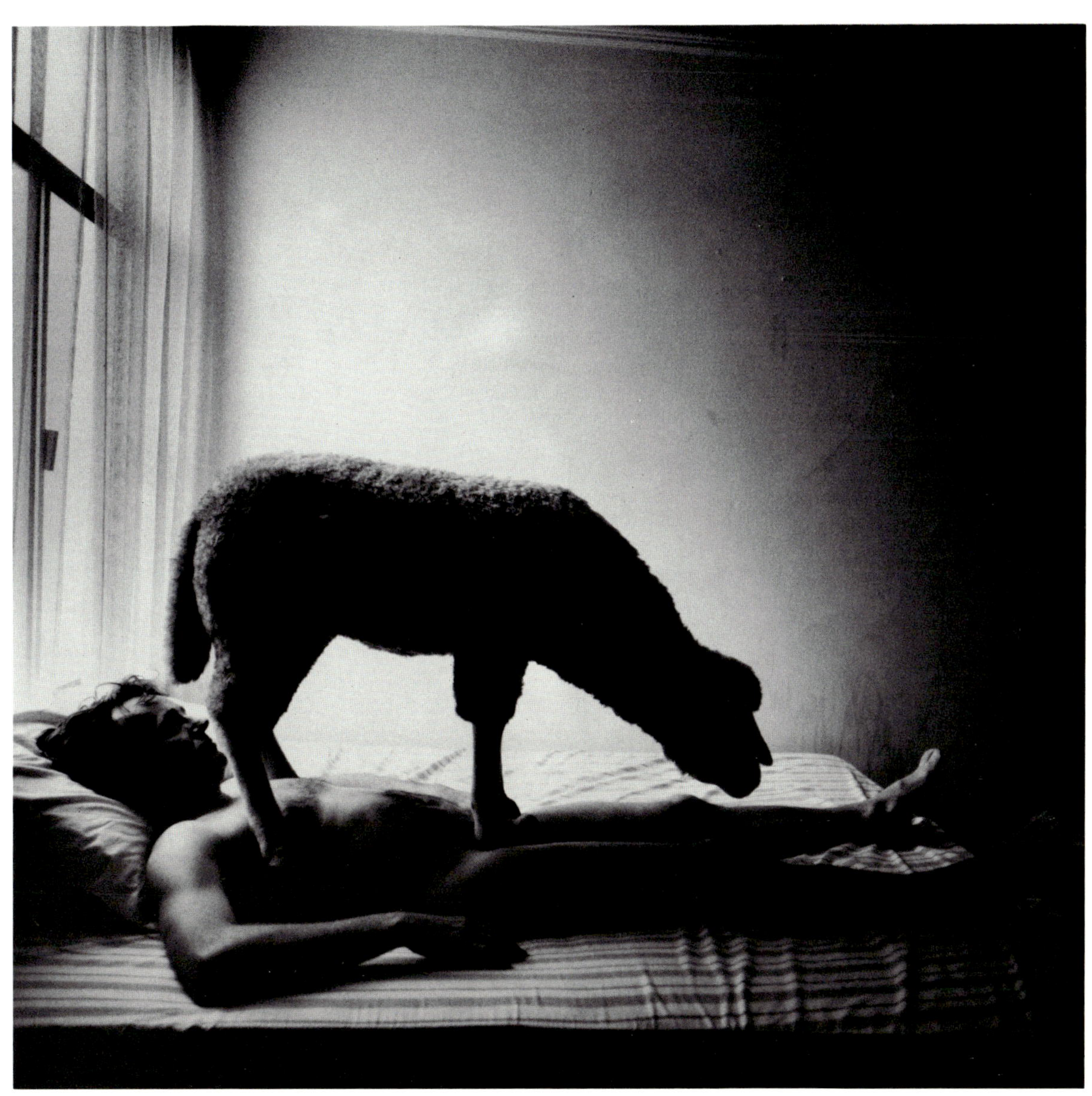

Gerald Marks and Pegasus, New York City

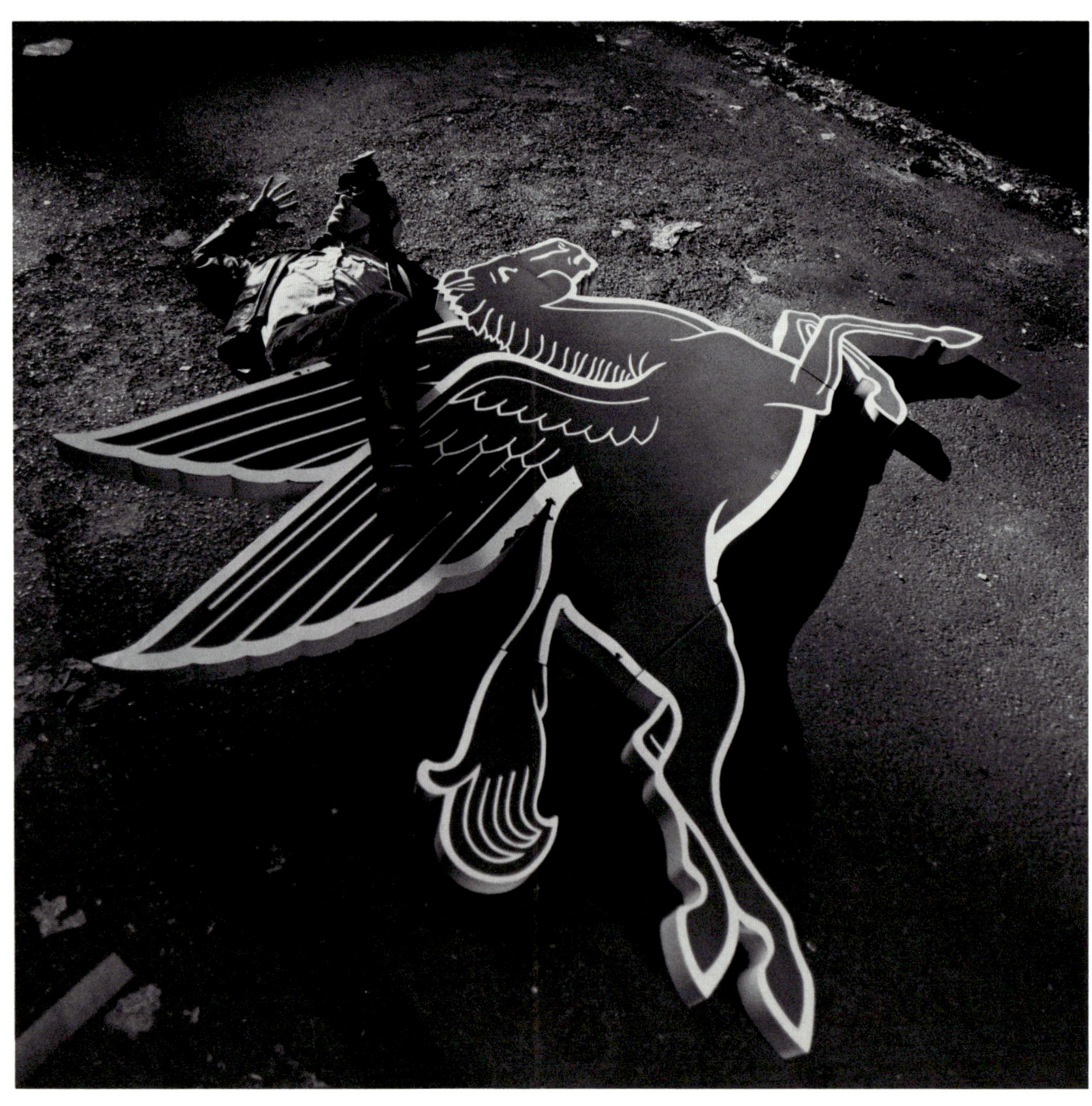

Paul Abels and Horse, Easthampton, New York

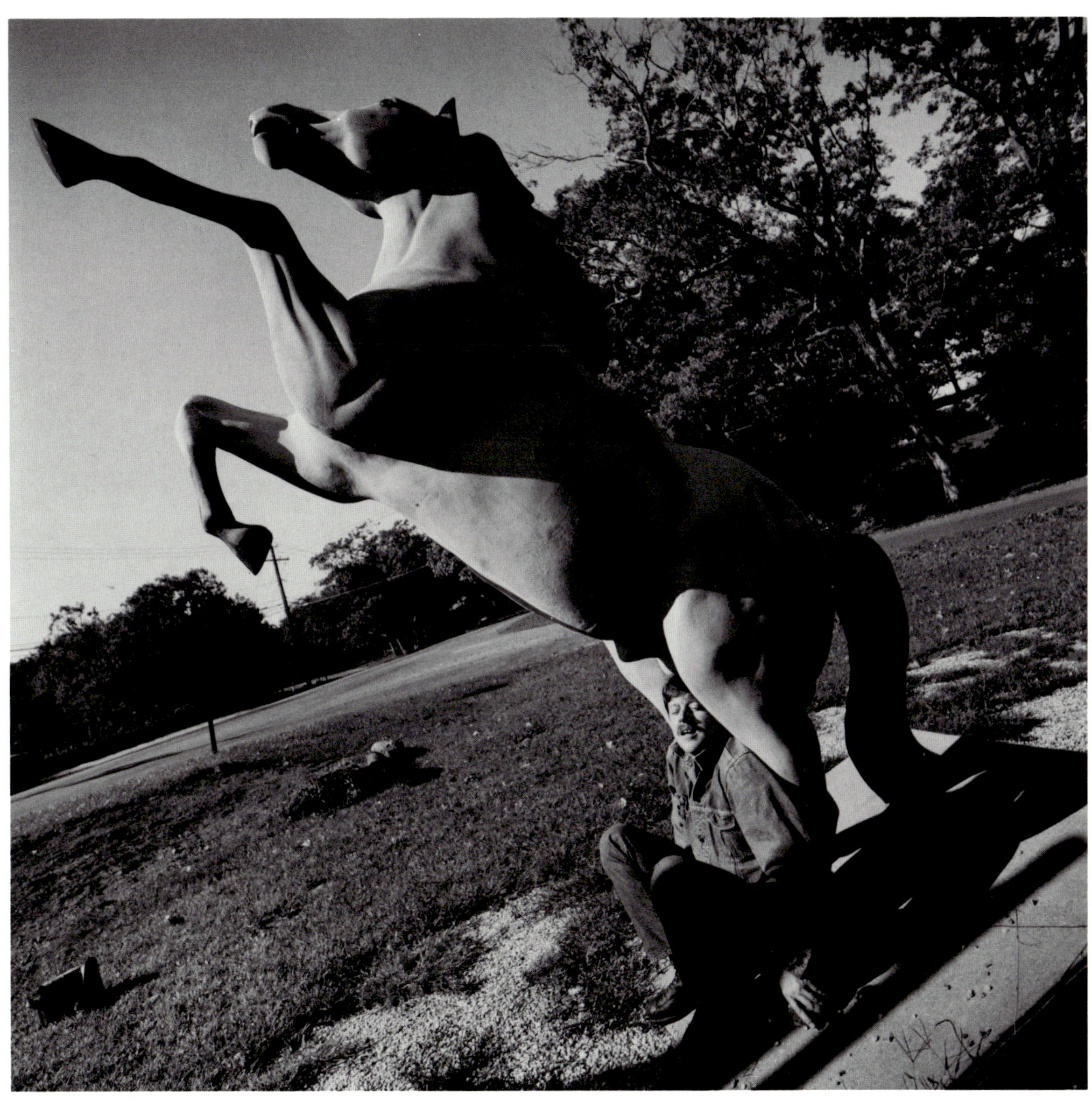

Antonio Miralda and Johanna, New York City

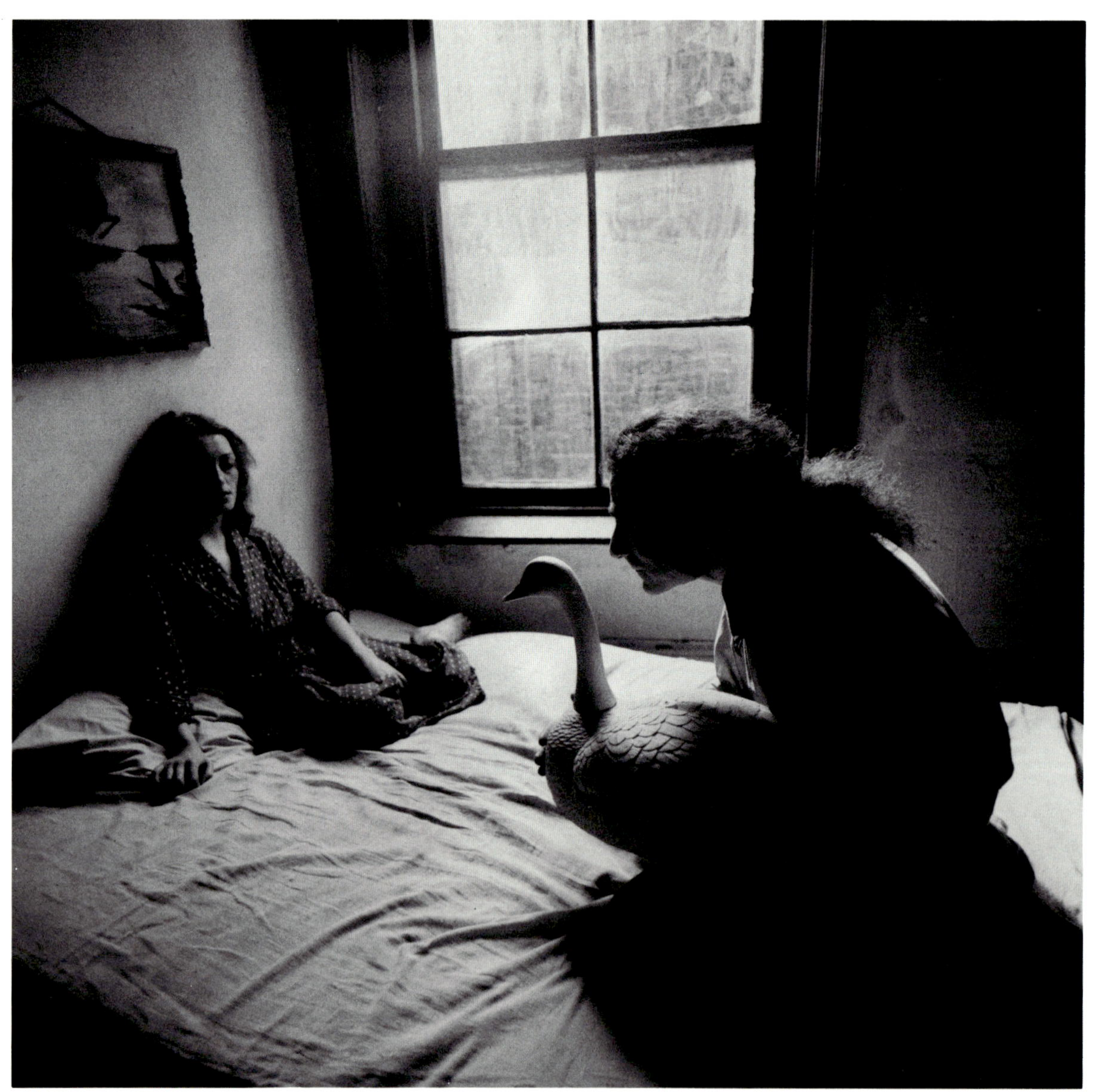

Giancarlo Bastianoni and his Wife, Nassau, Bahamas

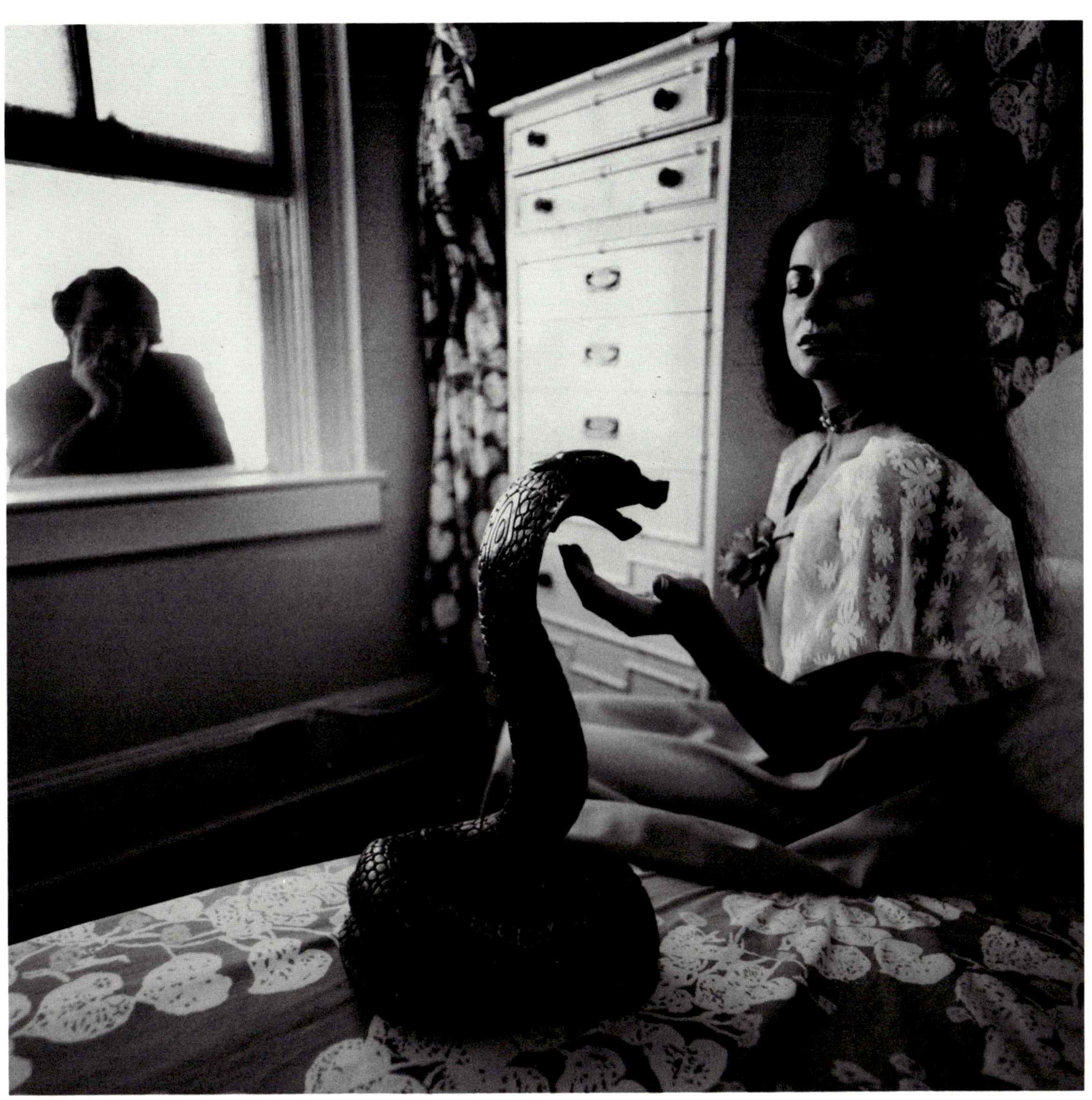

Man and Mickey Mouse, New York City

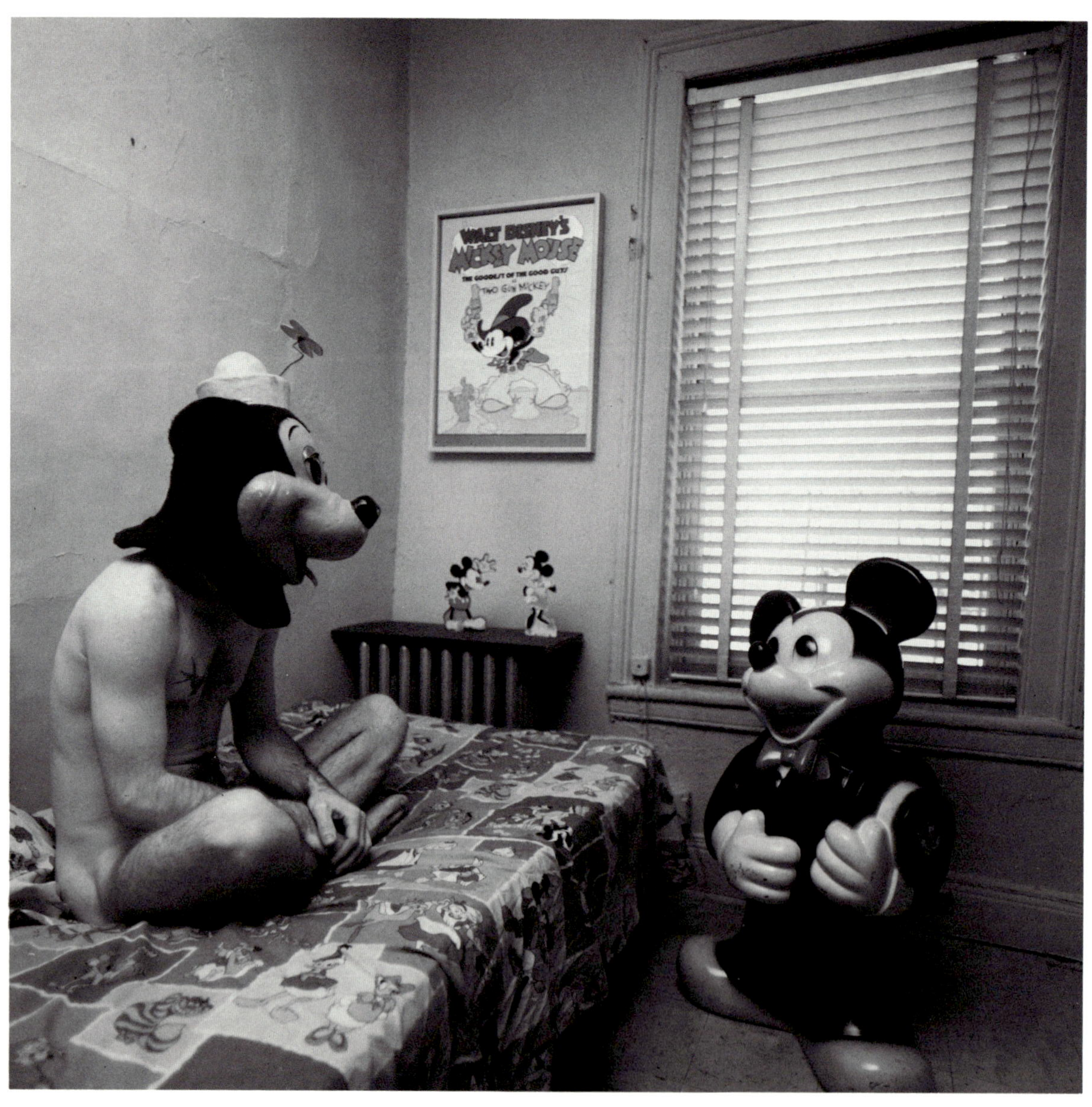

Charlotte Olds, Freeville, New York

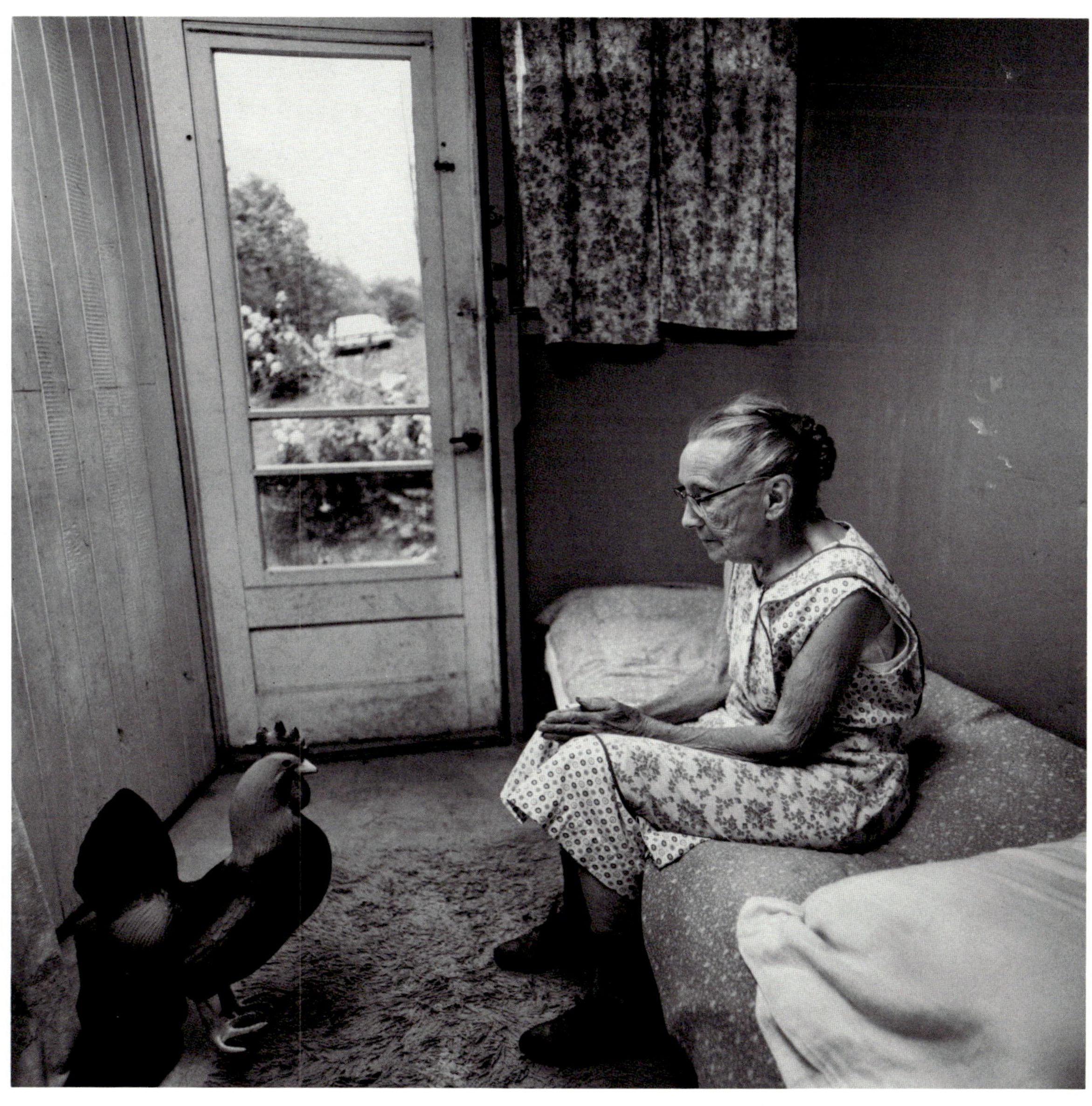

Mr. Merle Shoop, Van Etten, New York

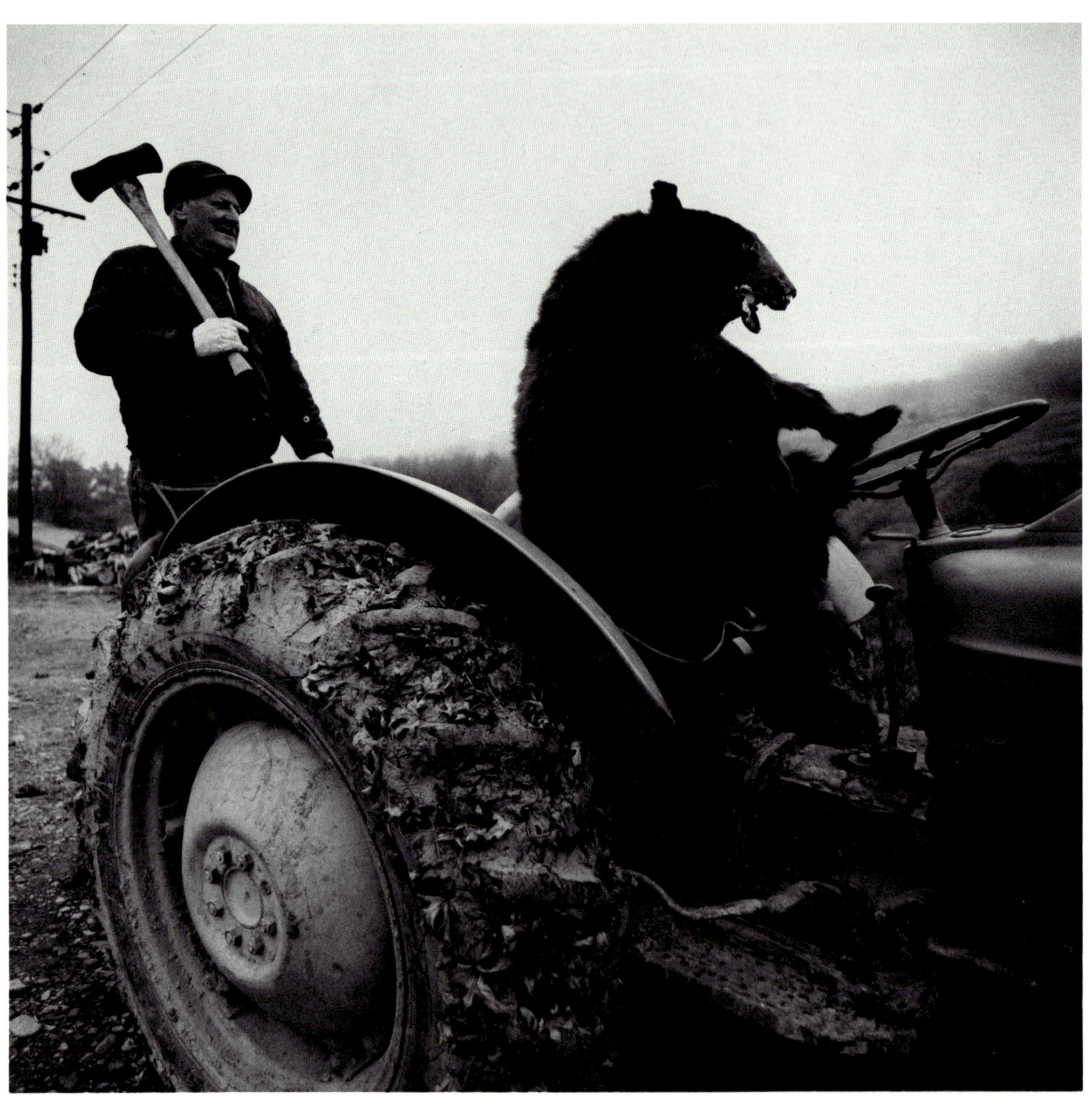

Mrs. Merle Shoop, Van Etten, New York

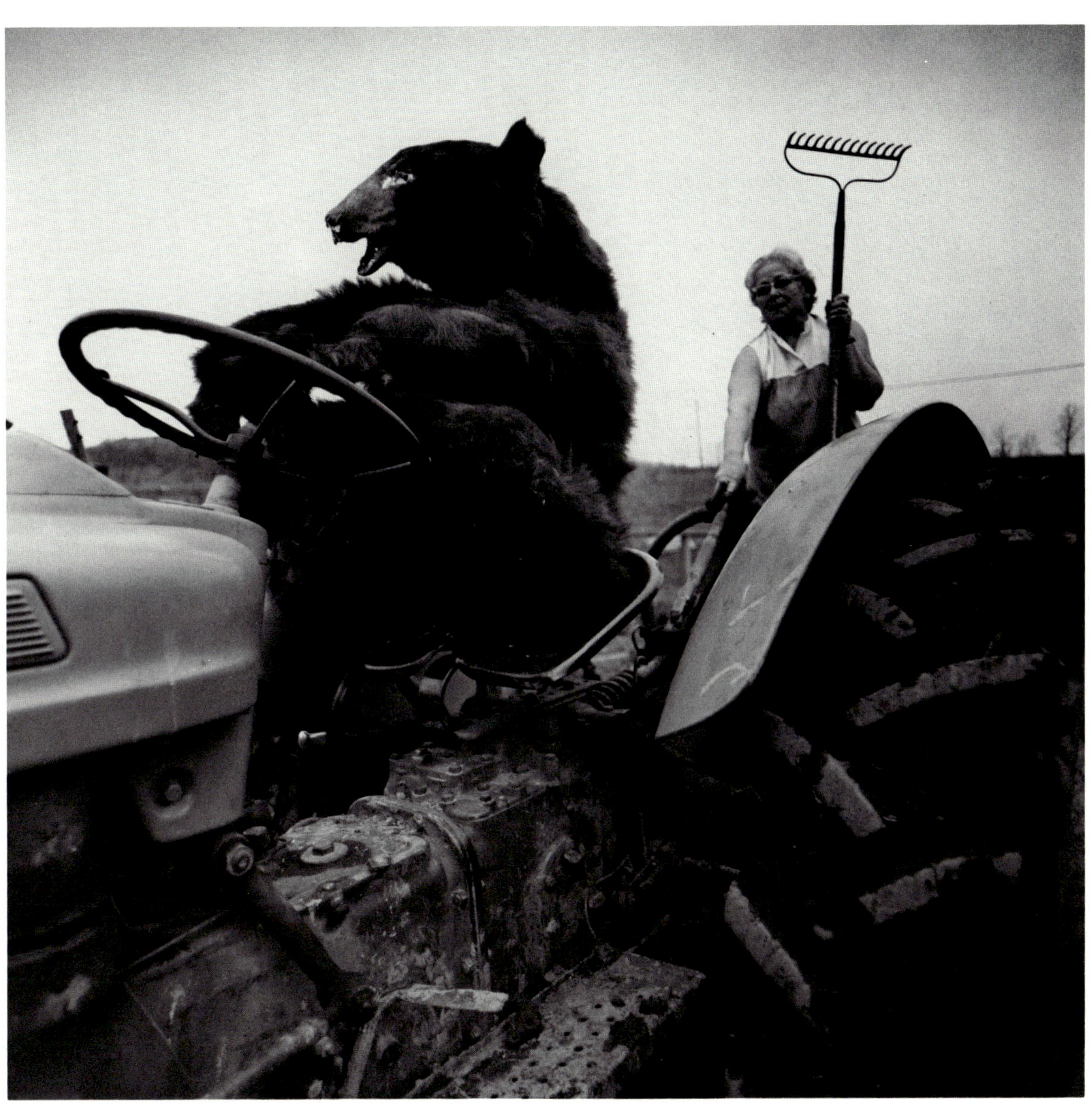

DOMESTIC SCENES

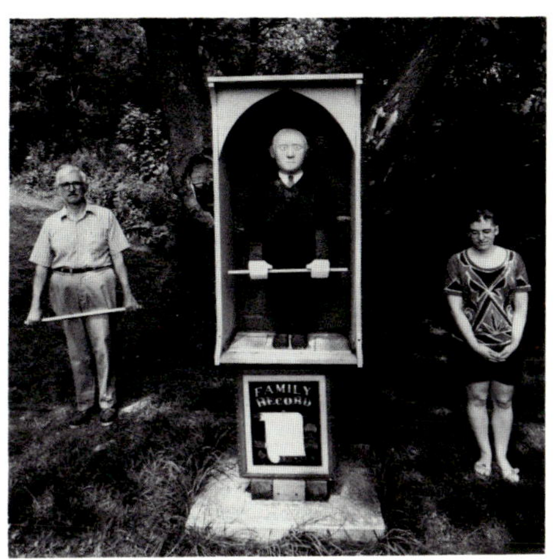

Mother and son, Princeton, New Jersey

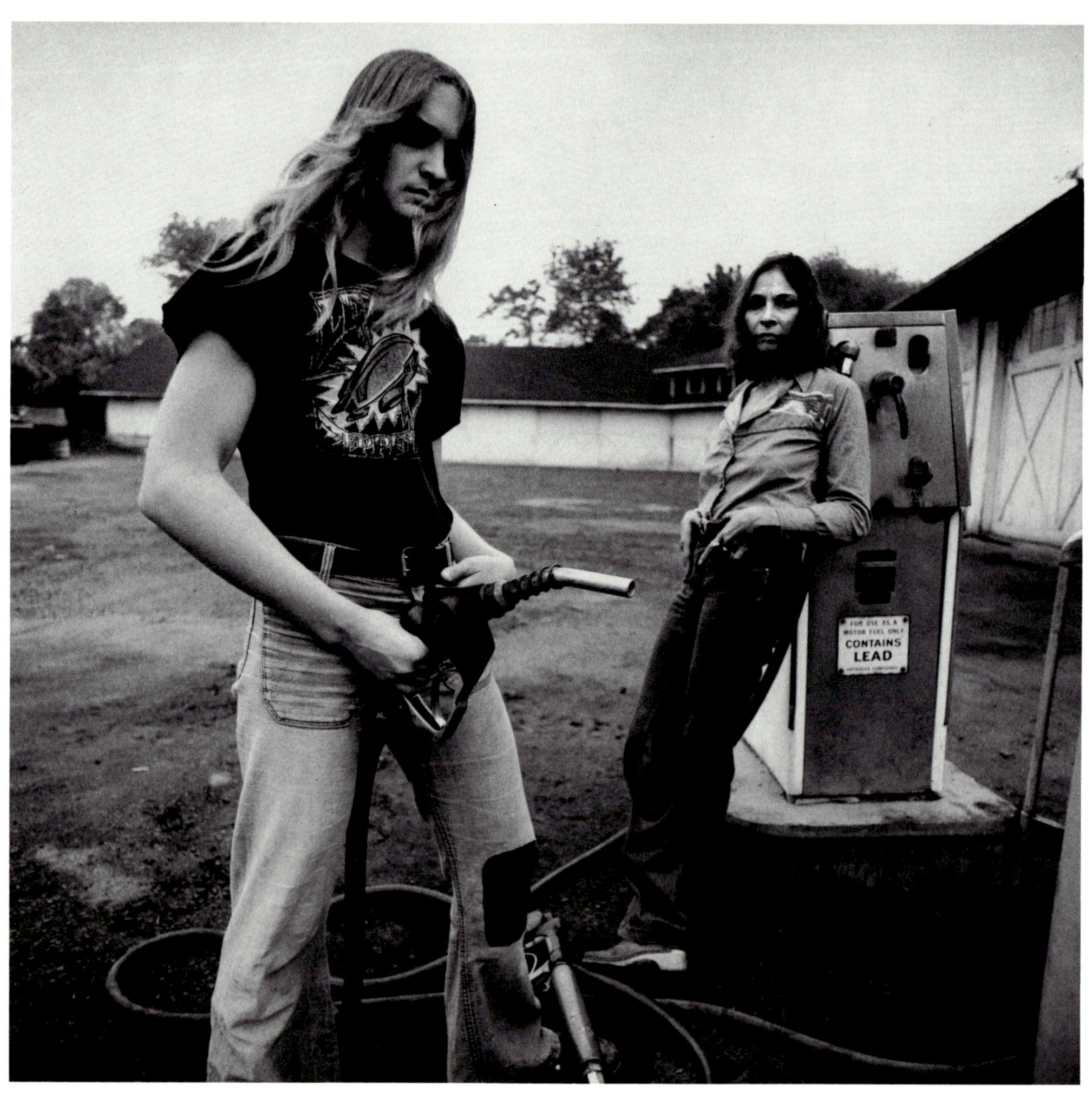

Brother and sister, Montauk, New York

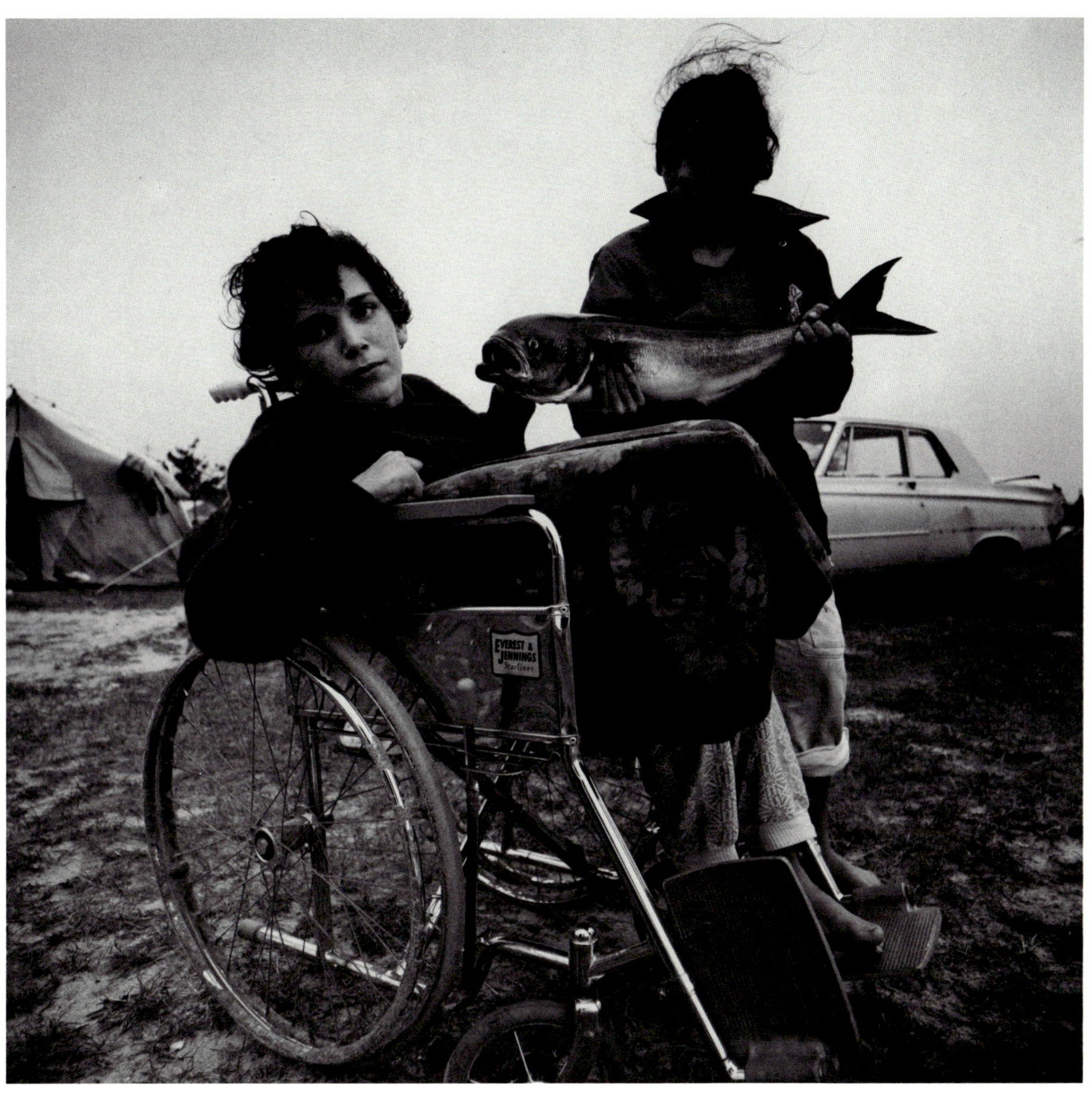

Hannah Stuart and her Mother, Sag Harbor, New York

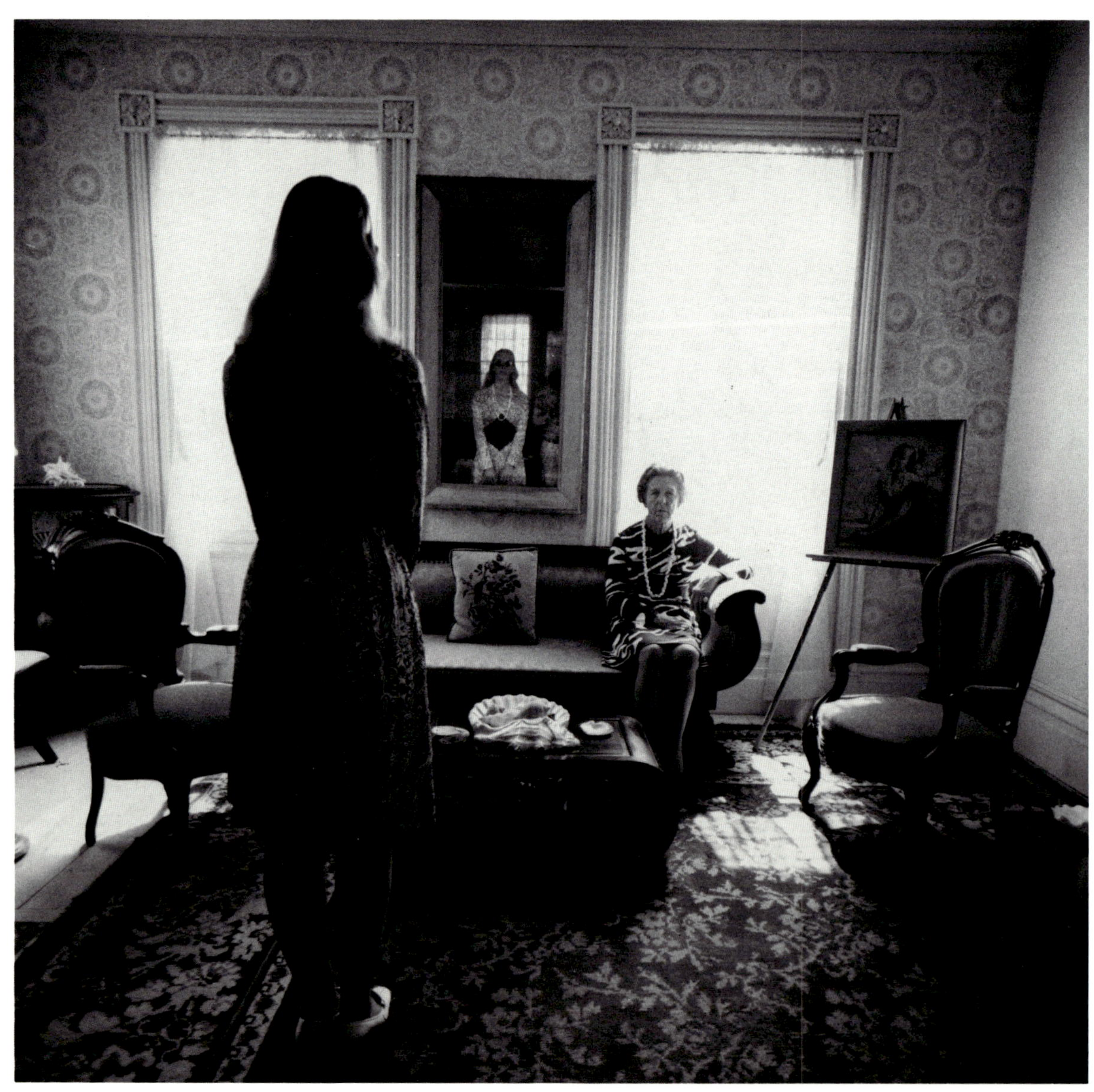

Hannah Stuart and her Mother, Sag Harbor, New York

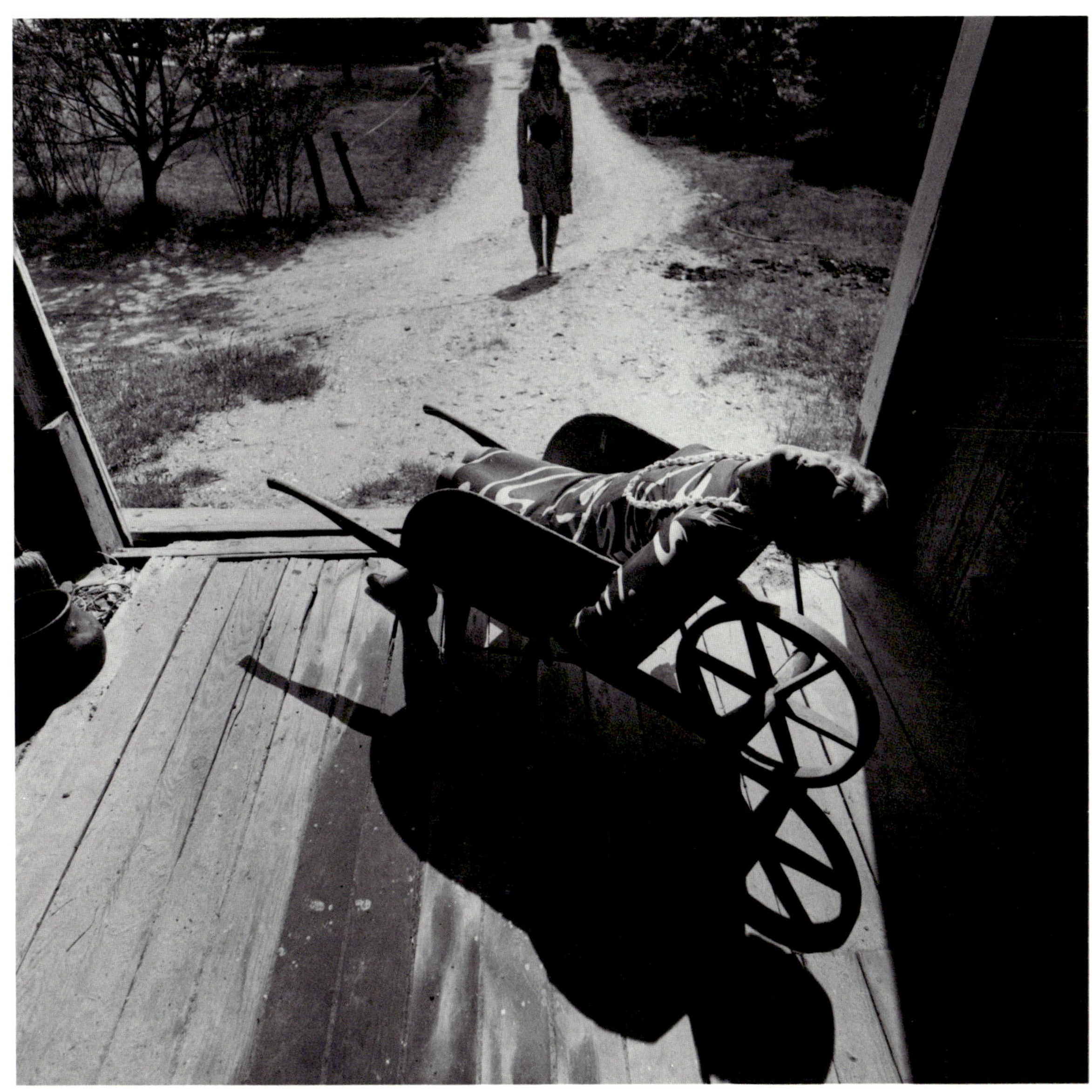

Pat Loud and her Children, New York City

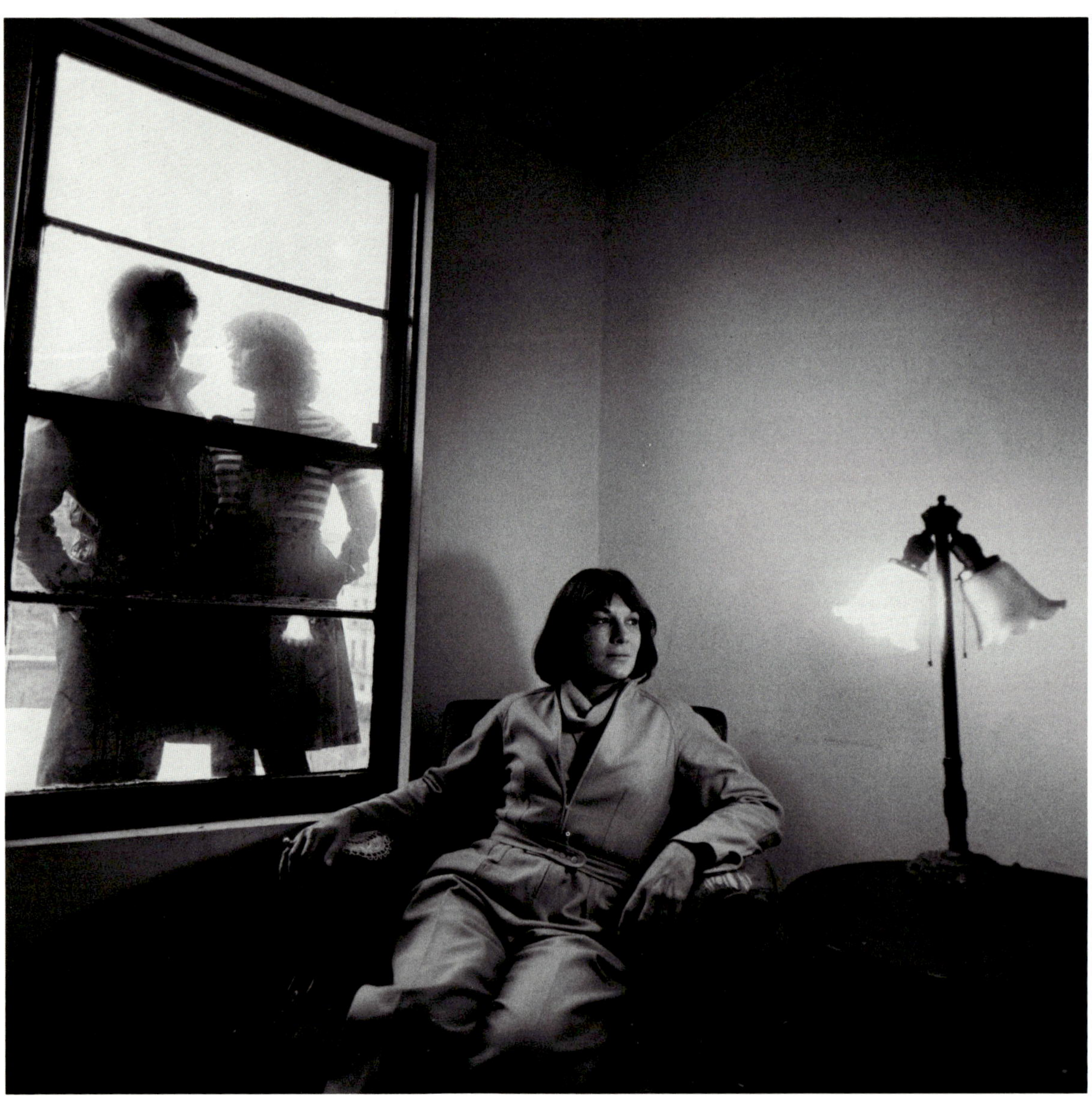

Mother, Son and Au Pair Girl, Houston, Texas

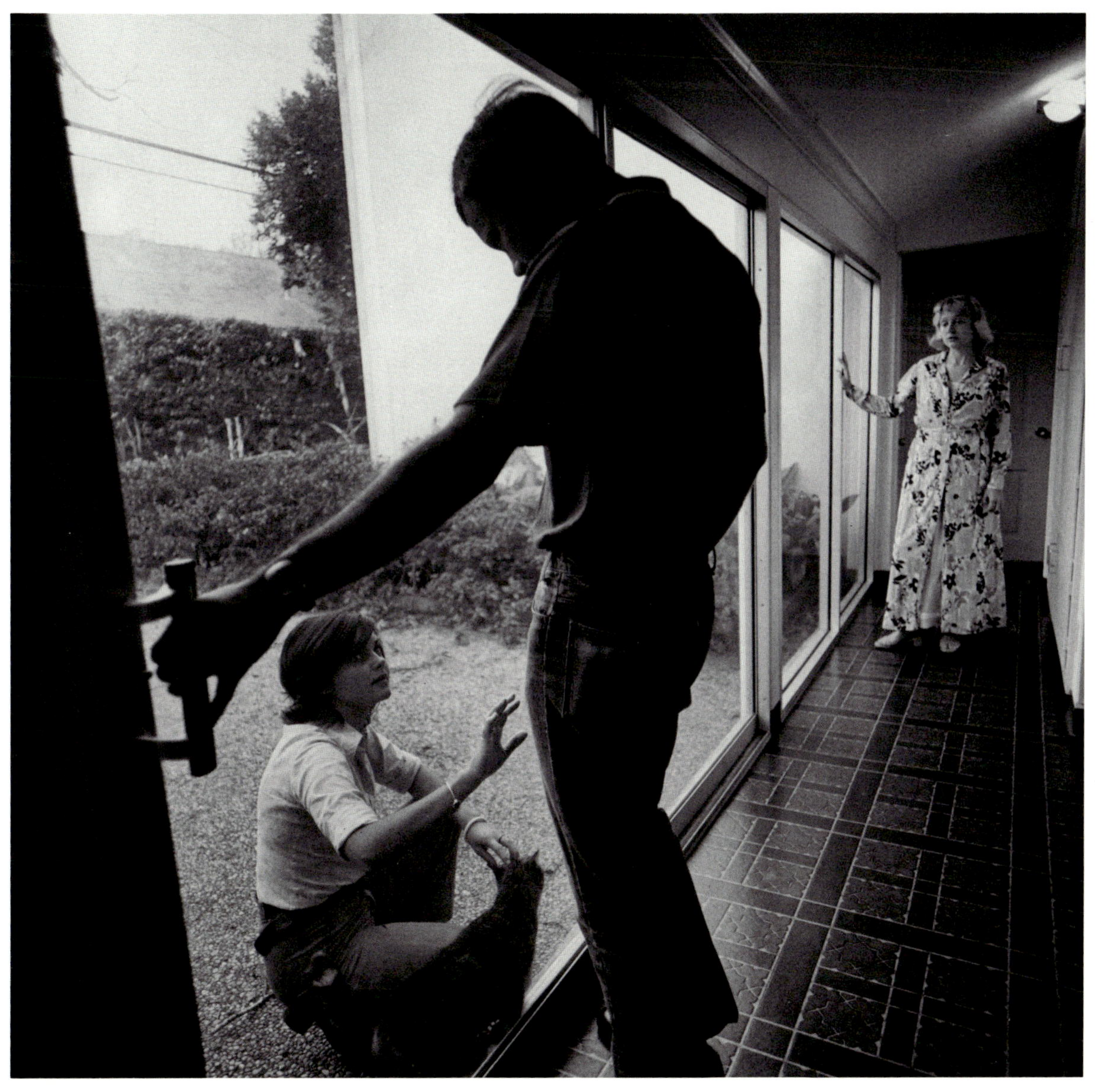

Ed and Judy Janowitz with William/Melissa, Nassau, Bahamas

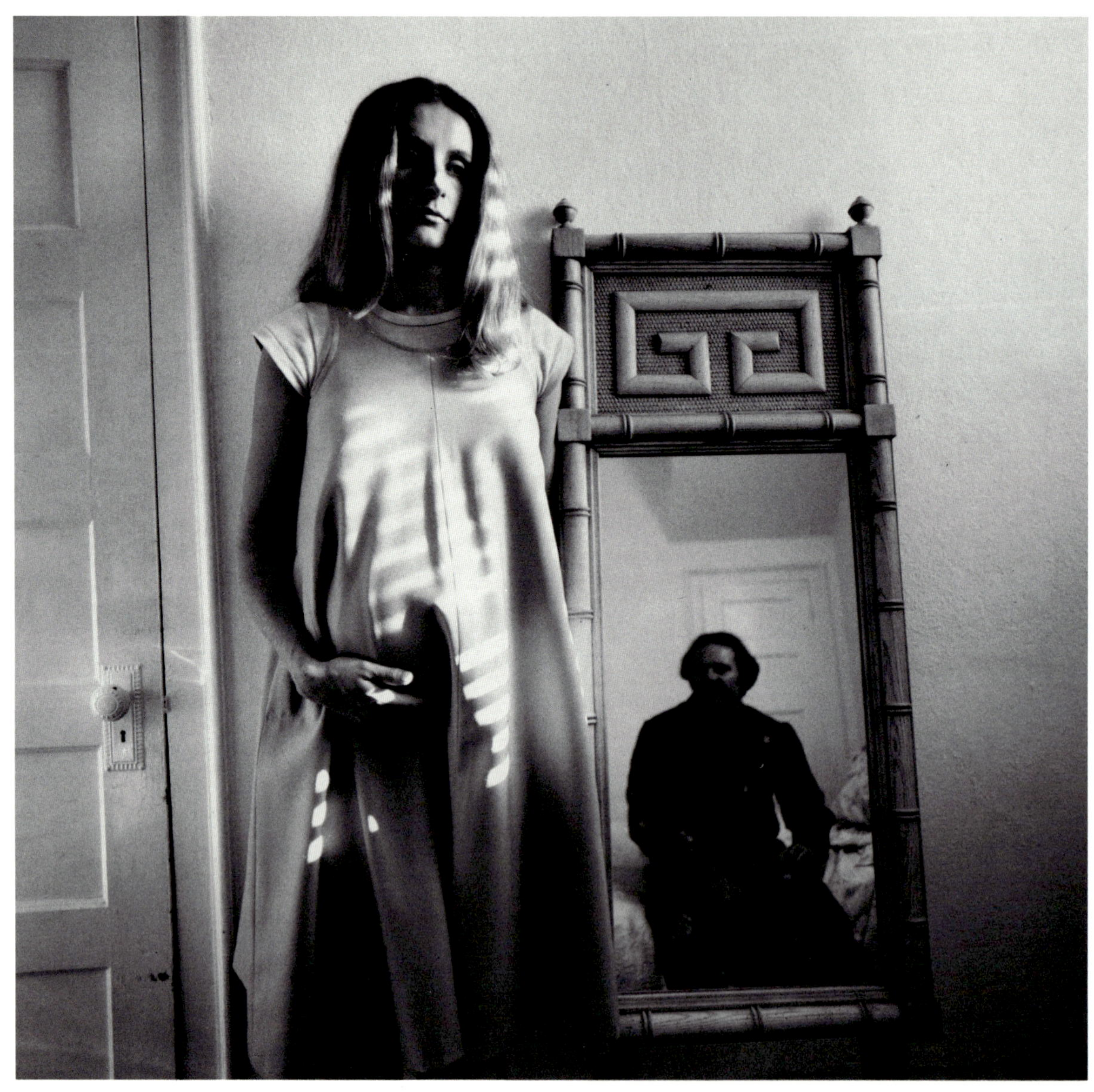

Jeffrey Costa and David, New York City

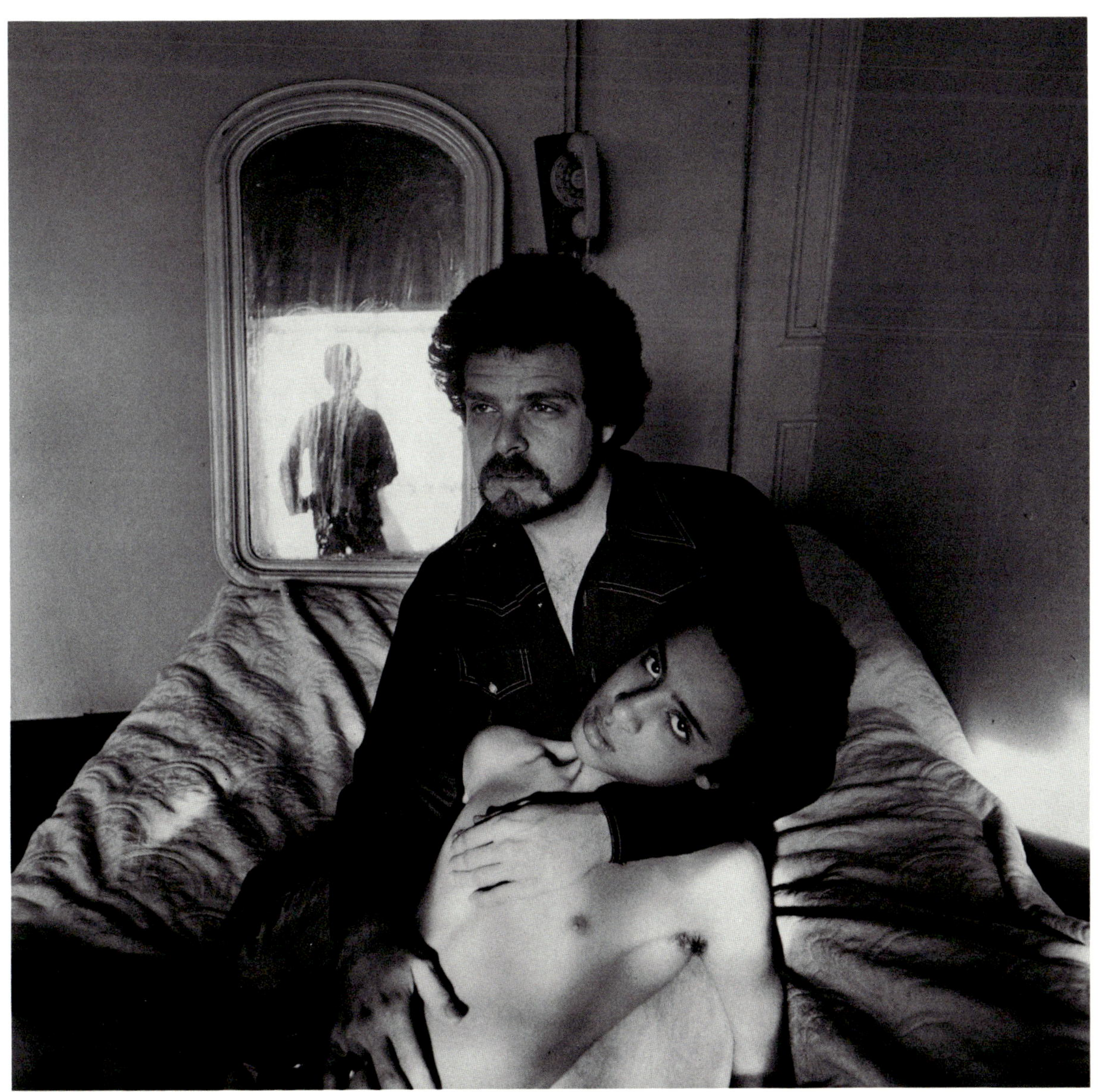

Andrew Singer and his Mother, New York City

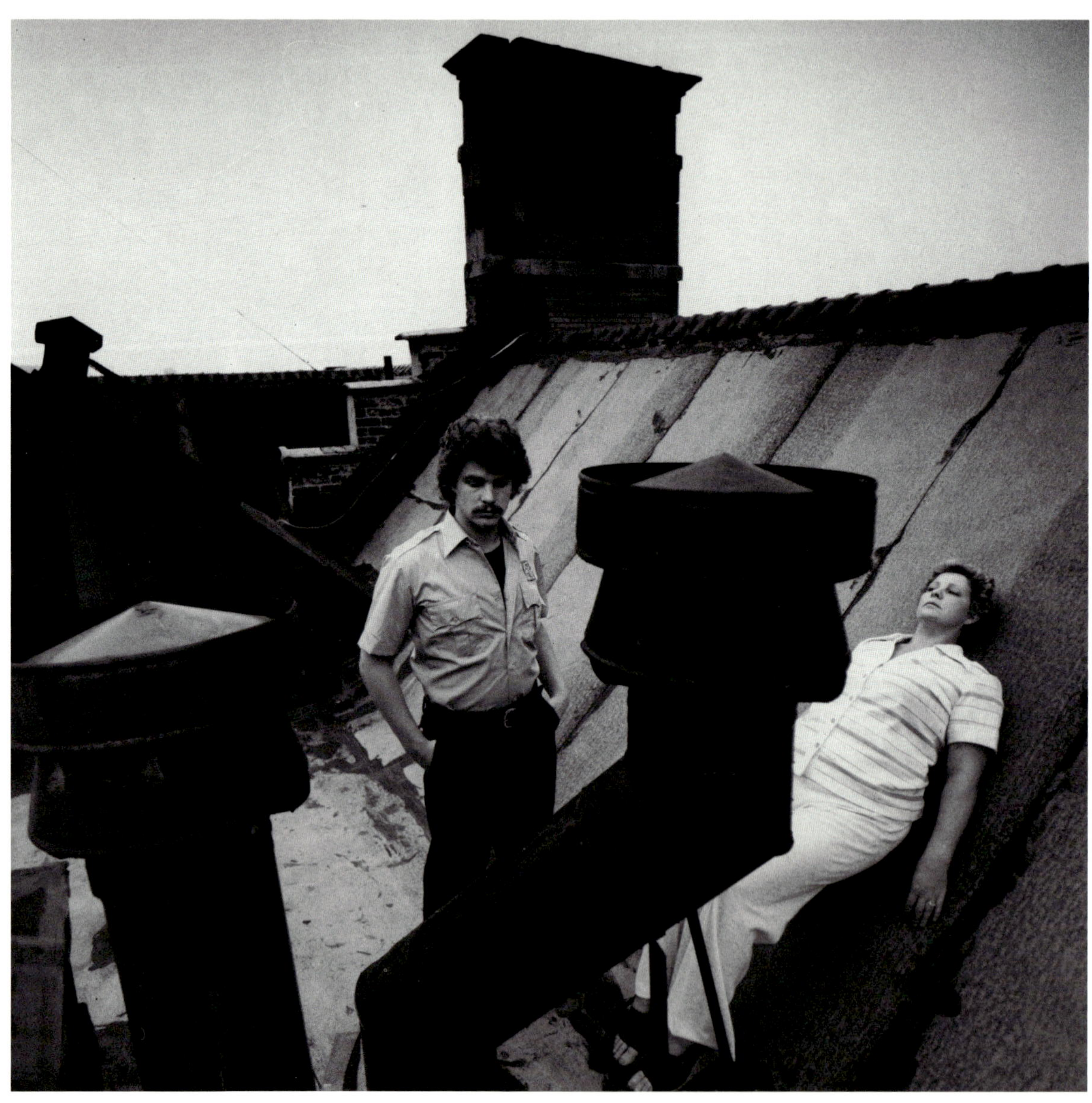

Bruce Hogenauer and his Mother, Bronx, New York

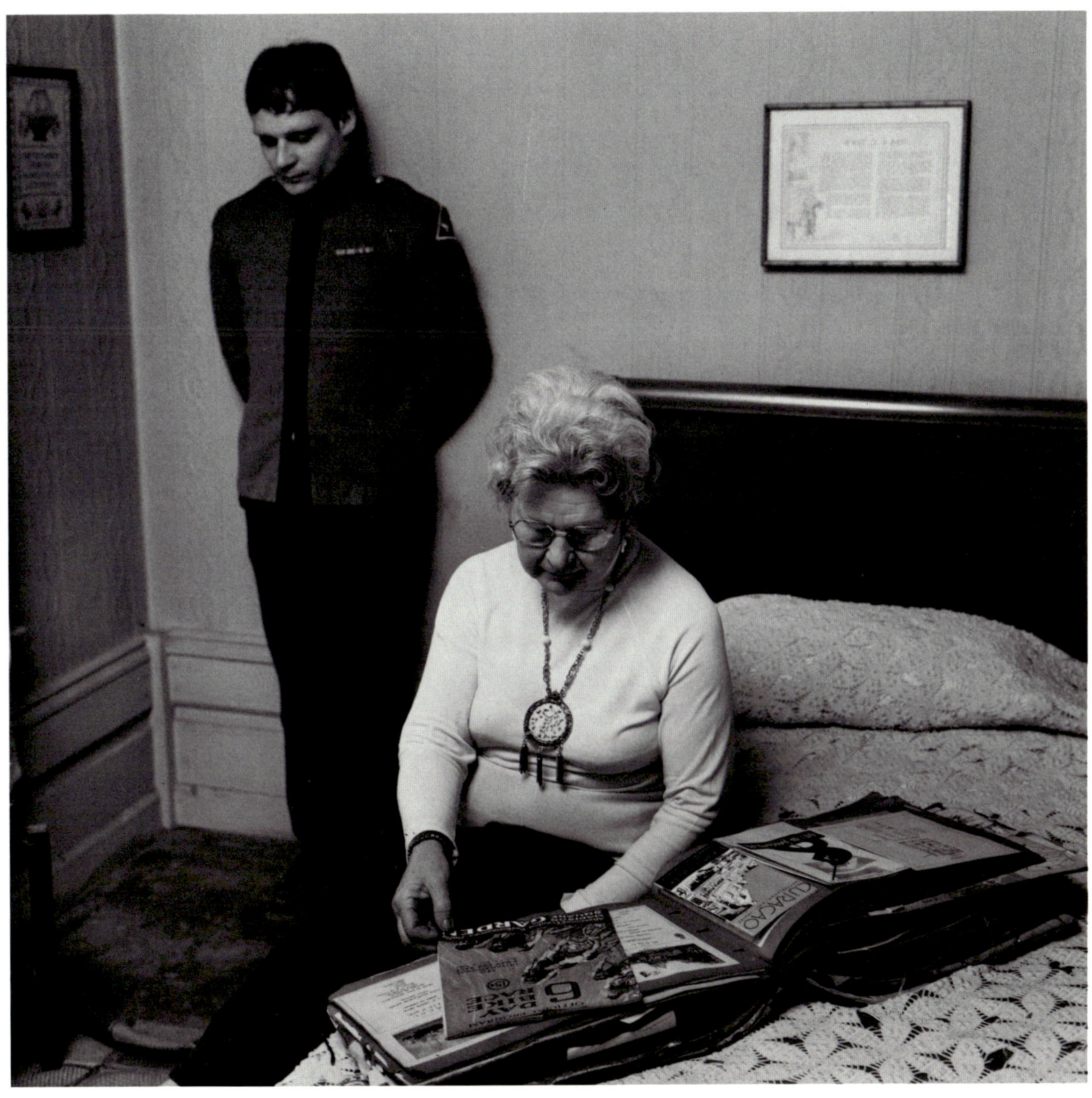

Jonathan Green and his Parents, New York City

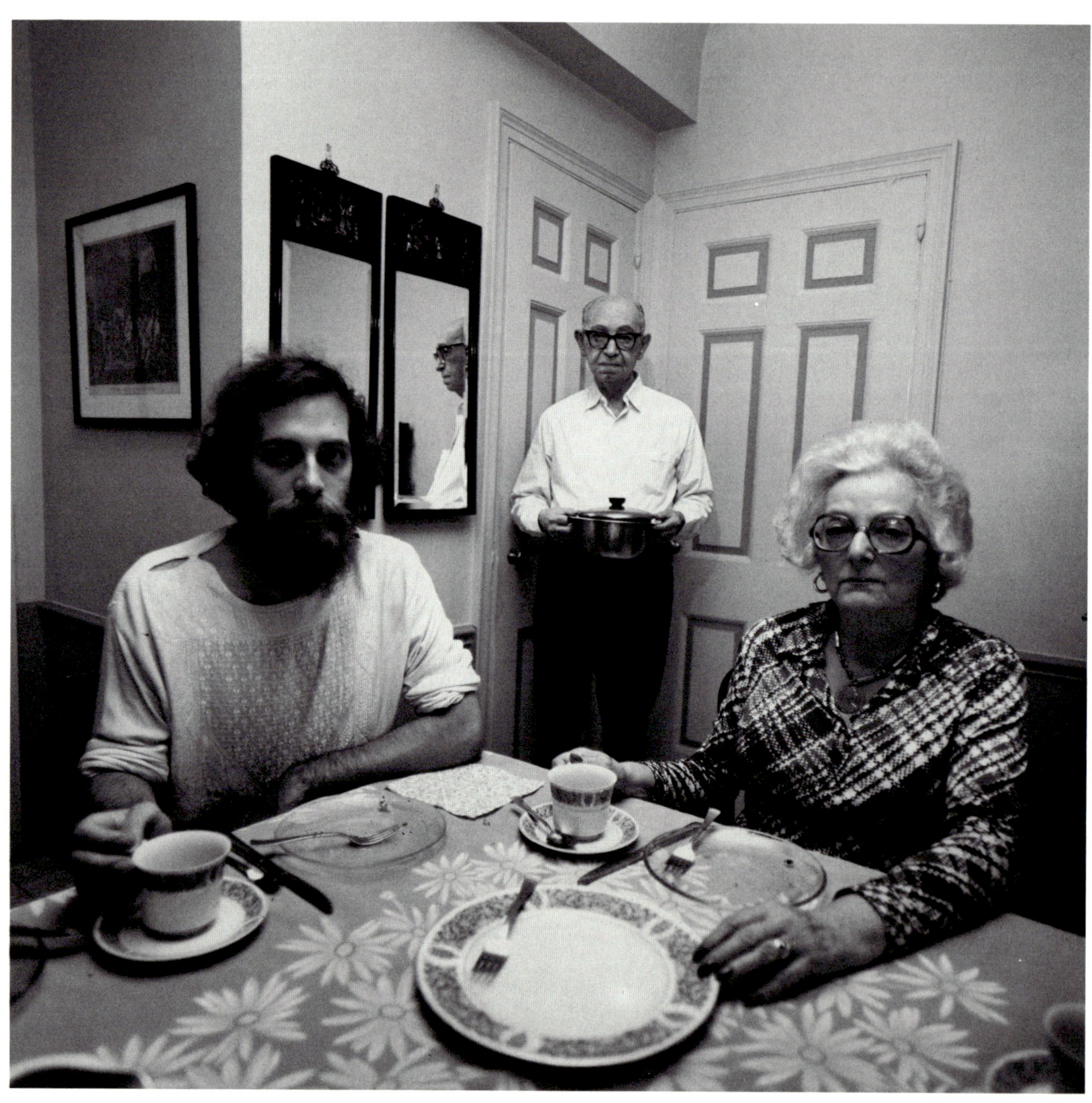

Arthur Young and his Daughter, Martha's Vineyard

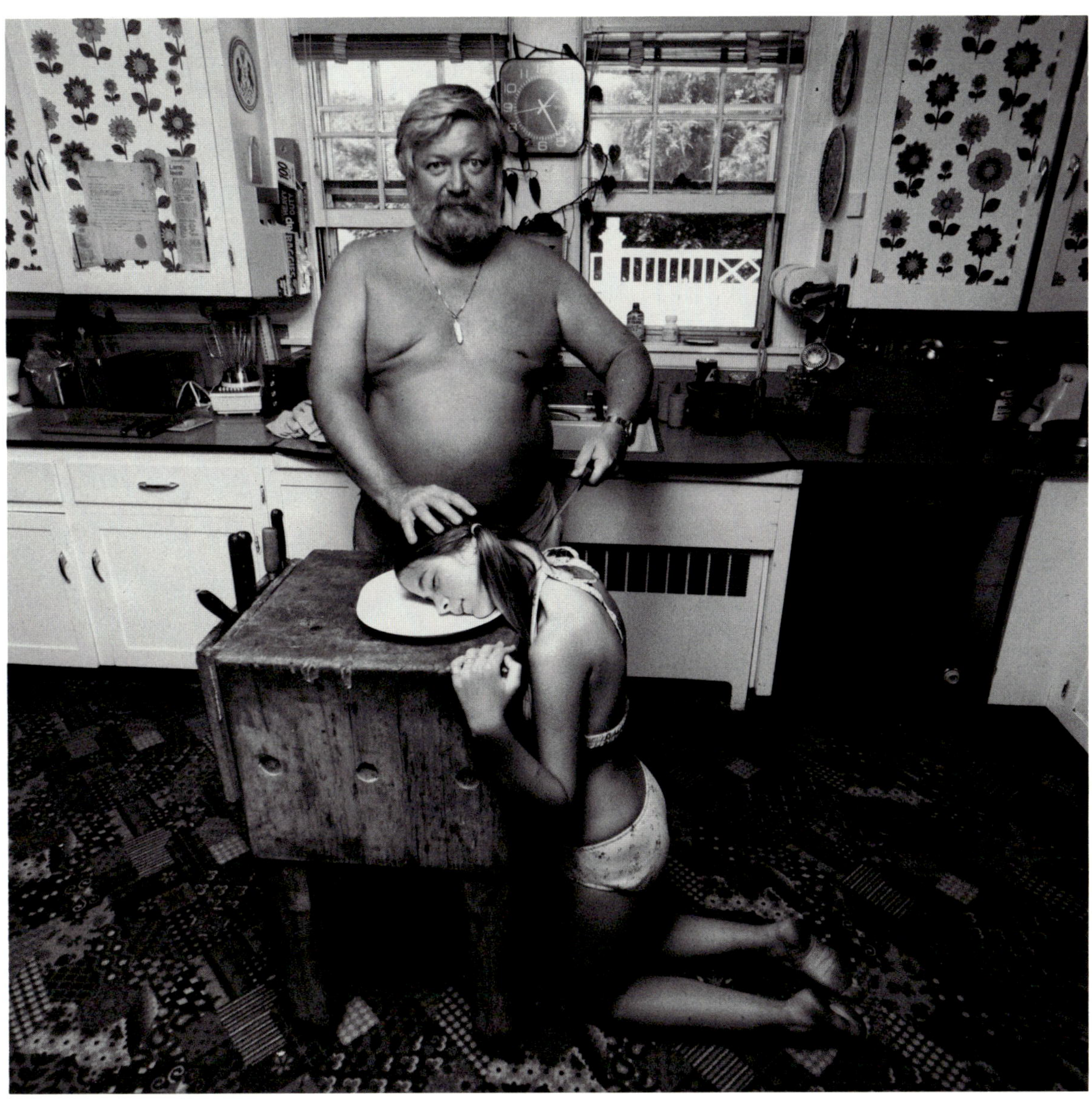

Ed Berman and his Mother, Brooklyn, New York

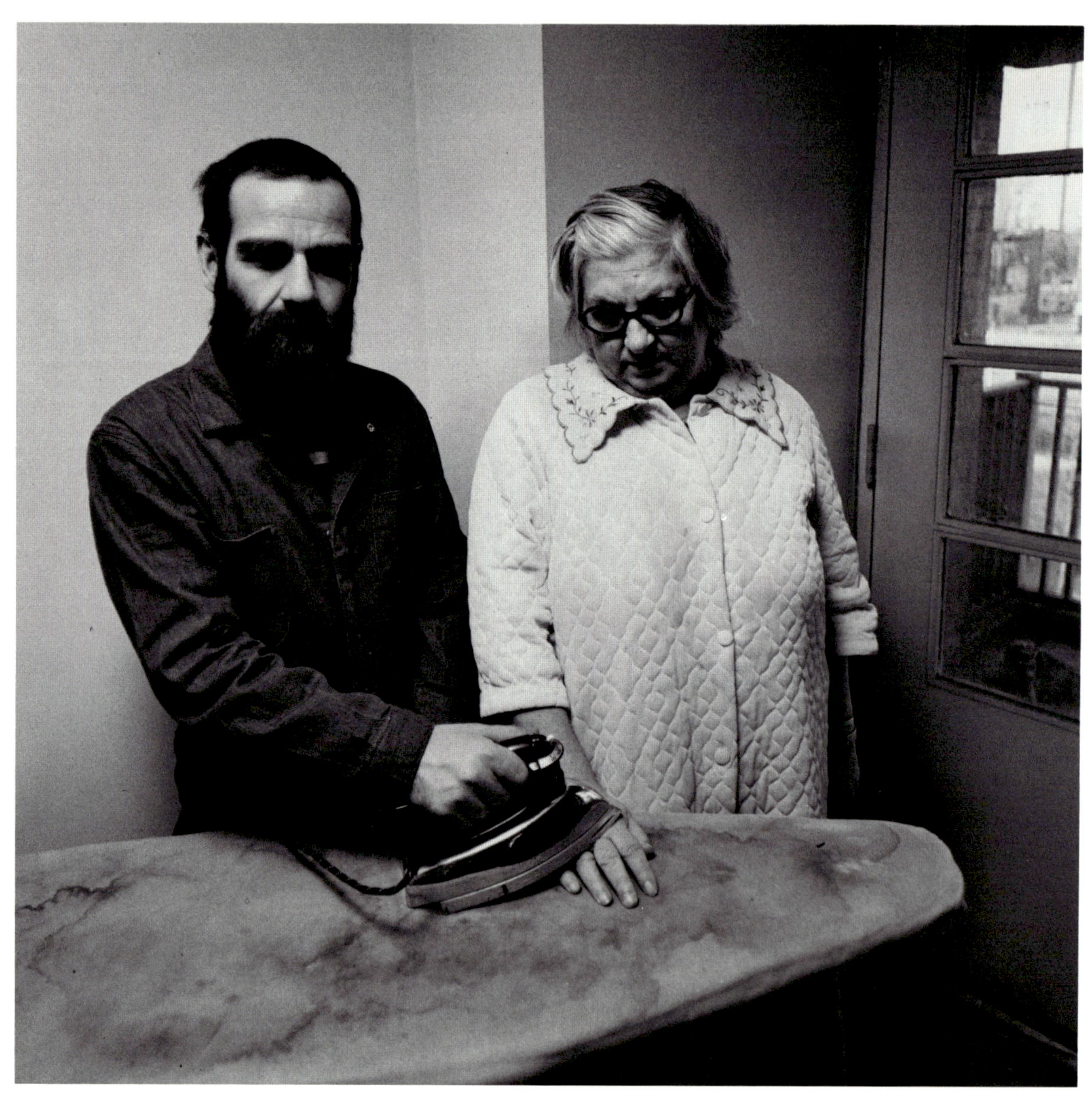

Dawn and Ethel, Scarborough, New York

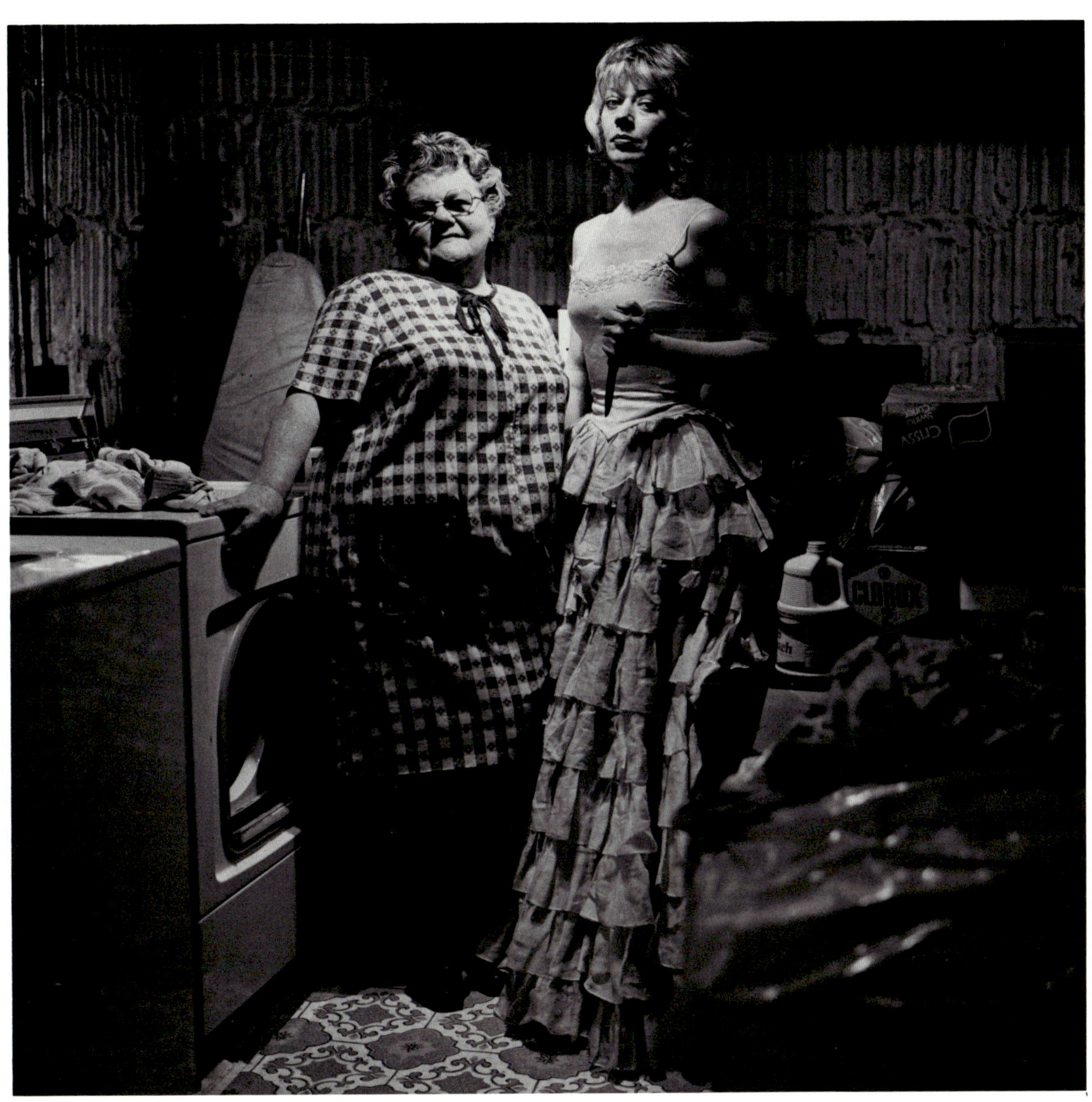

STAGE PROPERTIES

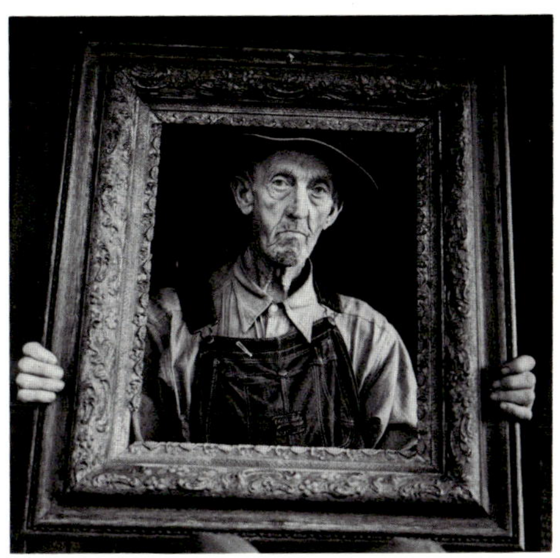

Larry Zimmerman with World's Fair Memoribilia, New York City

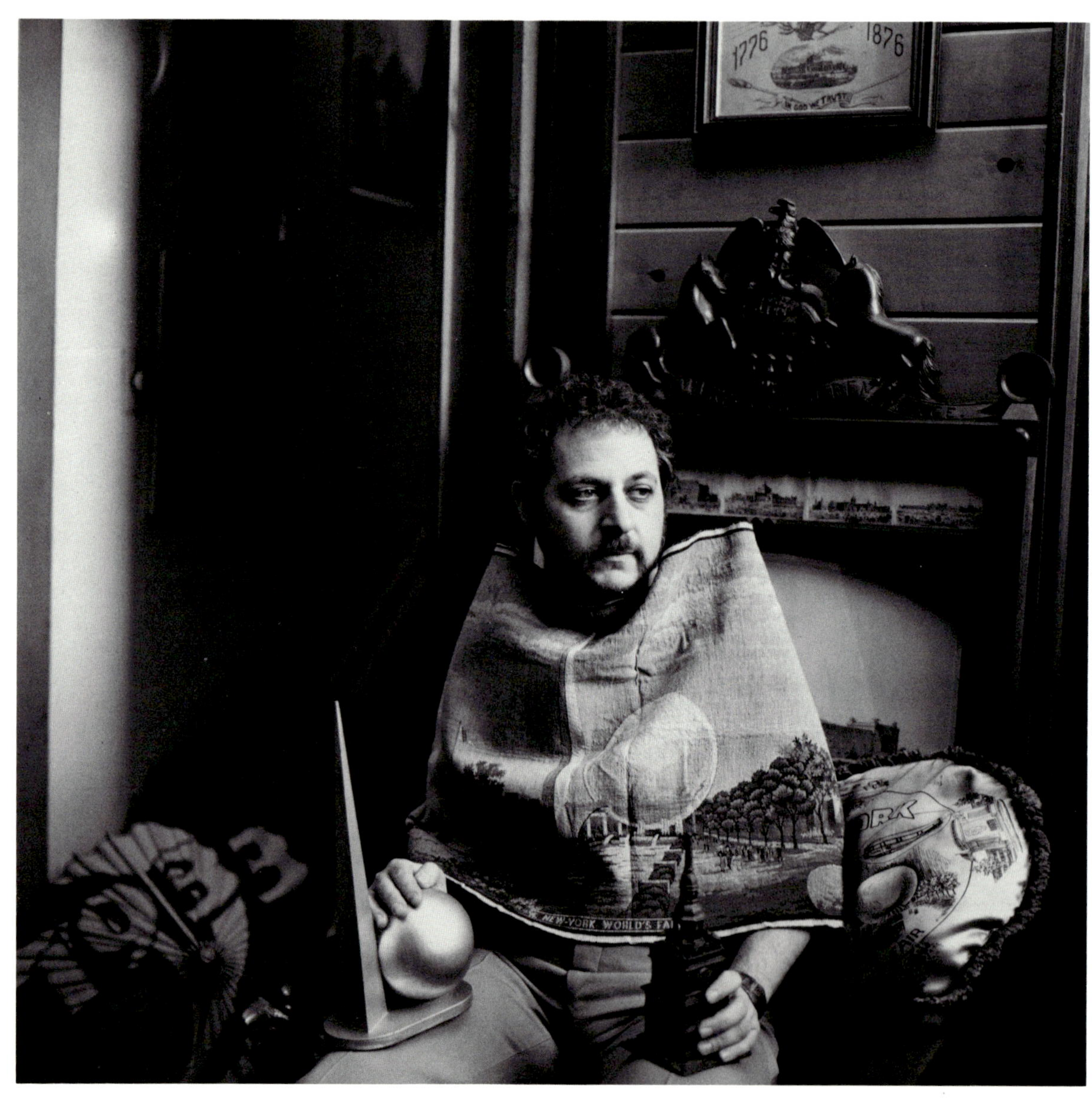

Sutherland McCalley, Curator, Yonkers, New York

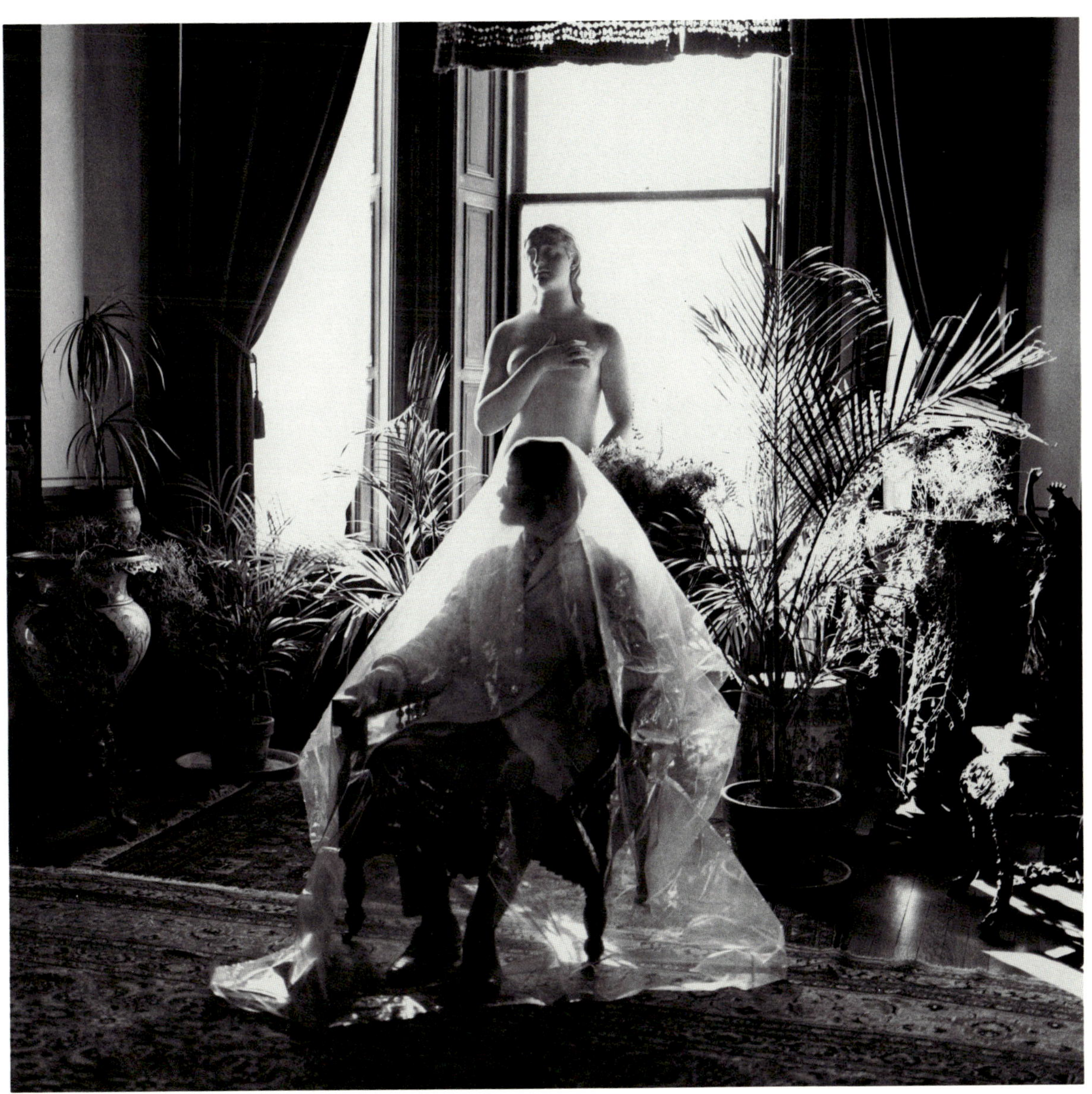

Attic in Ghost Town, Dillon, Colorado

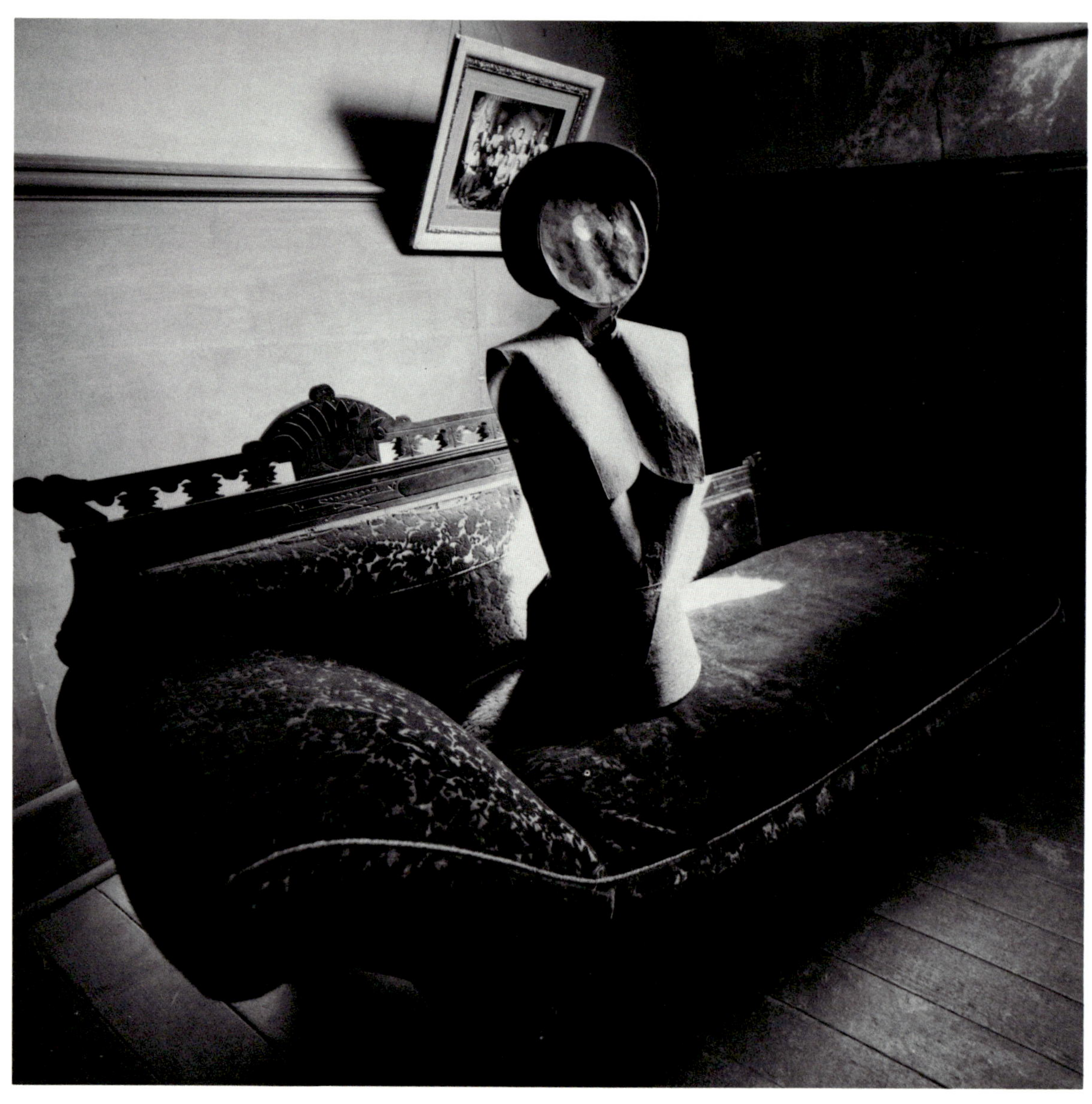

Mr. X., Clock Collector, New York City

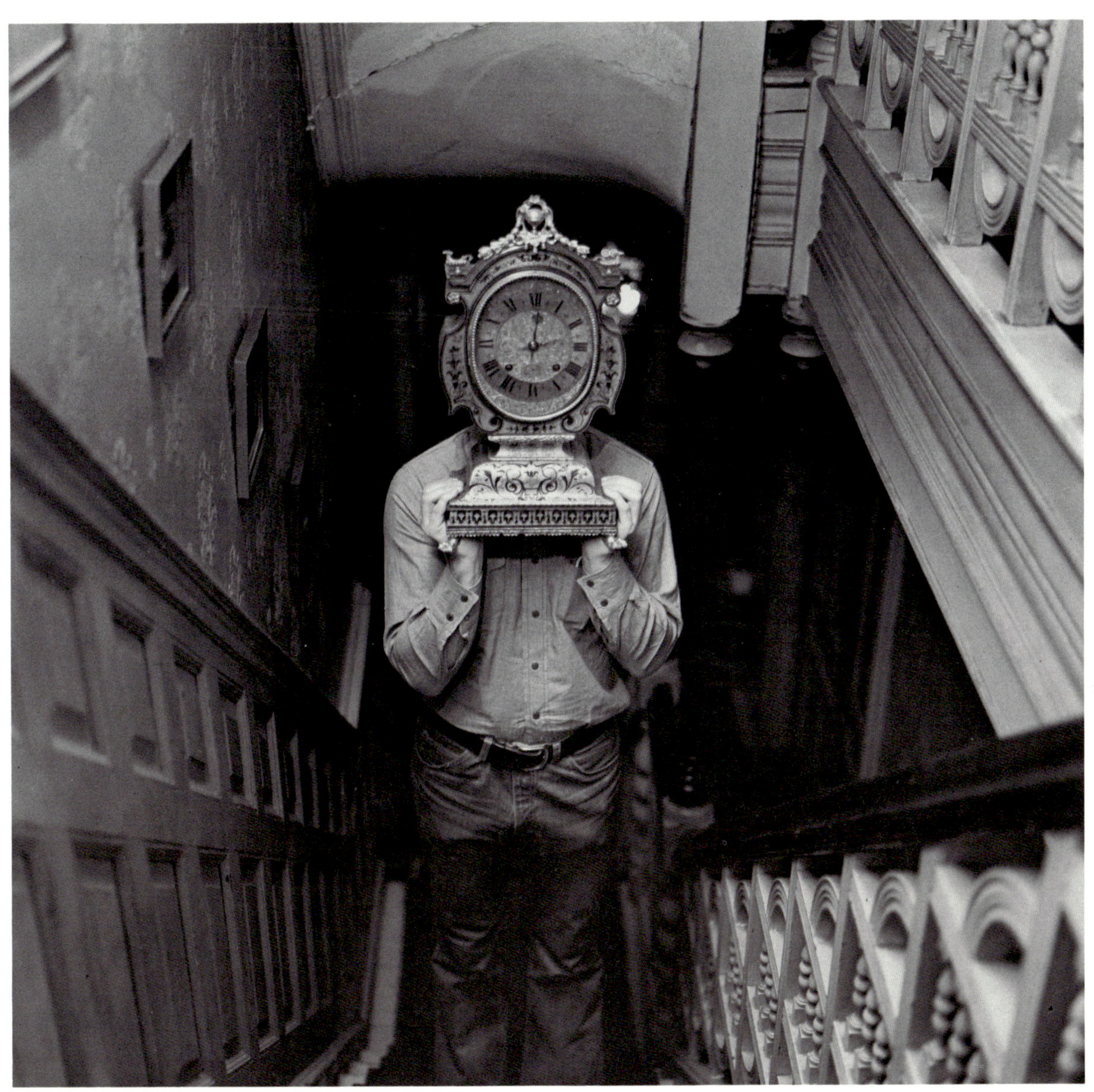

Elmer Kline and Marc Cohen, The Music Lesson, New York City

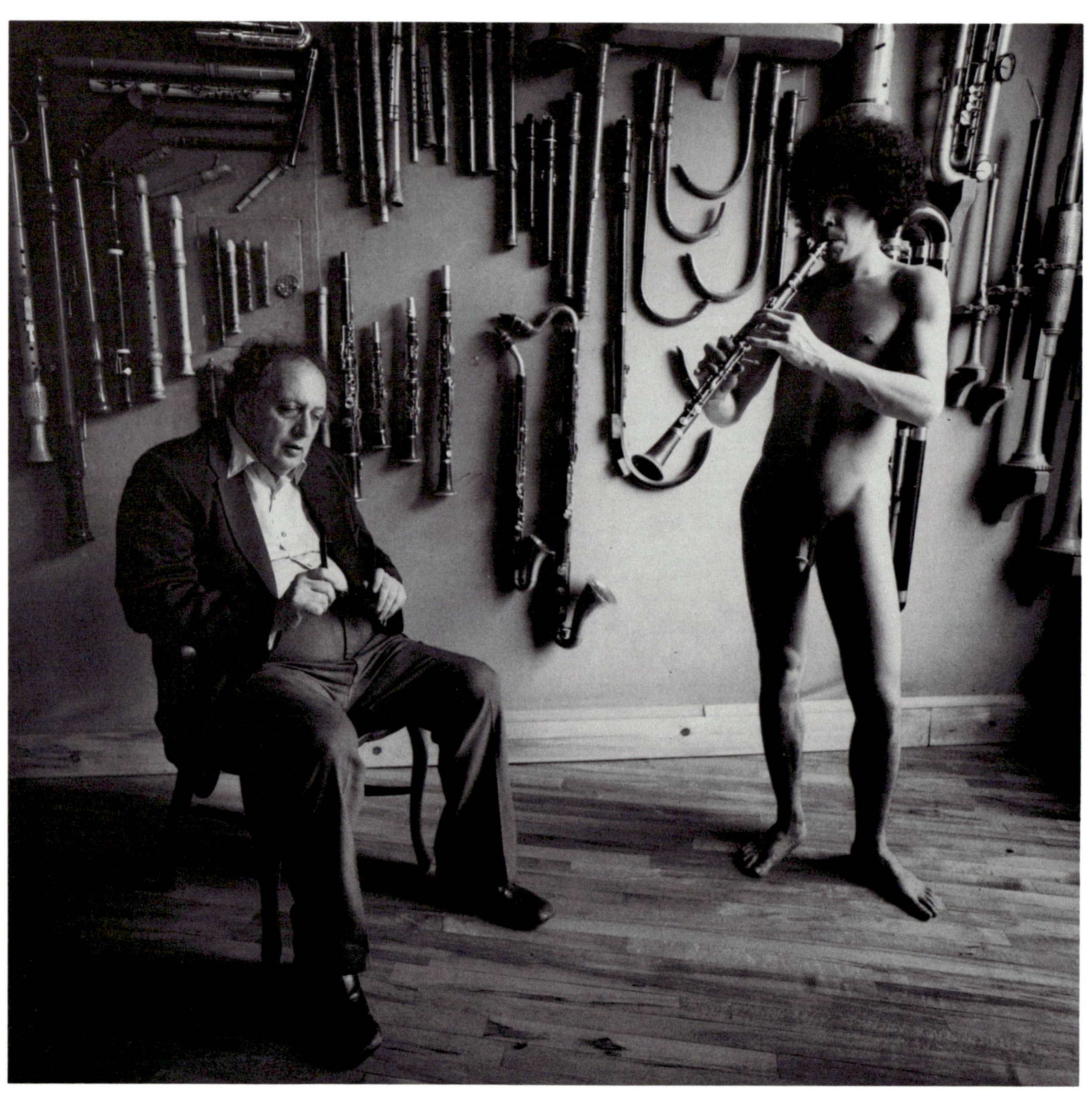

Augusto Machado with Cinemabilia, New York City

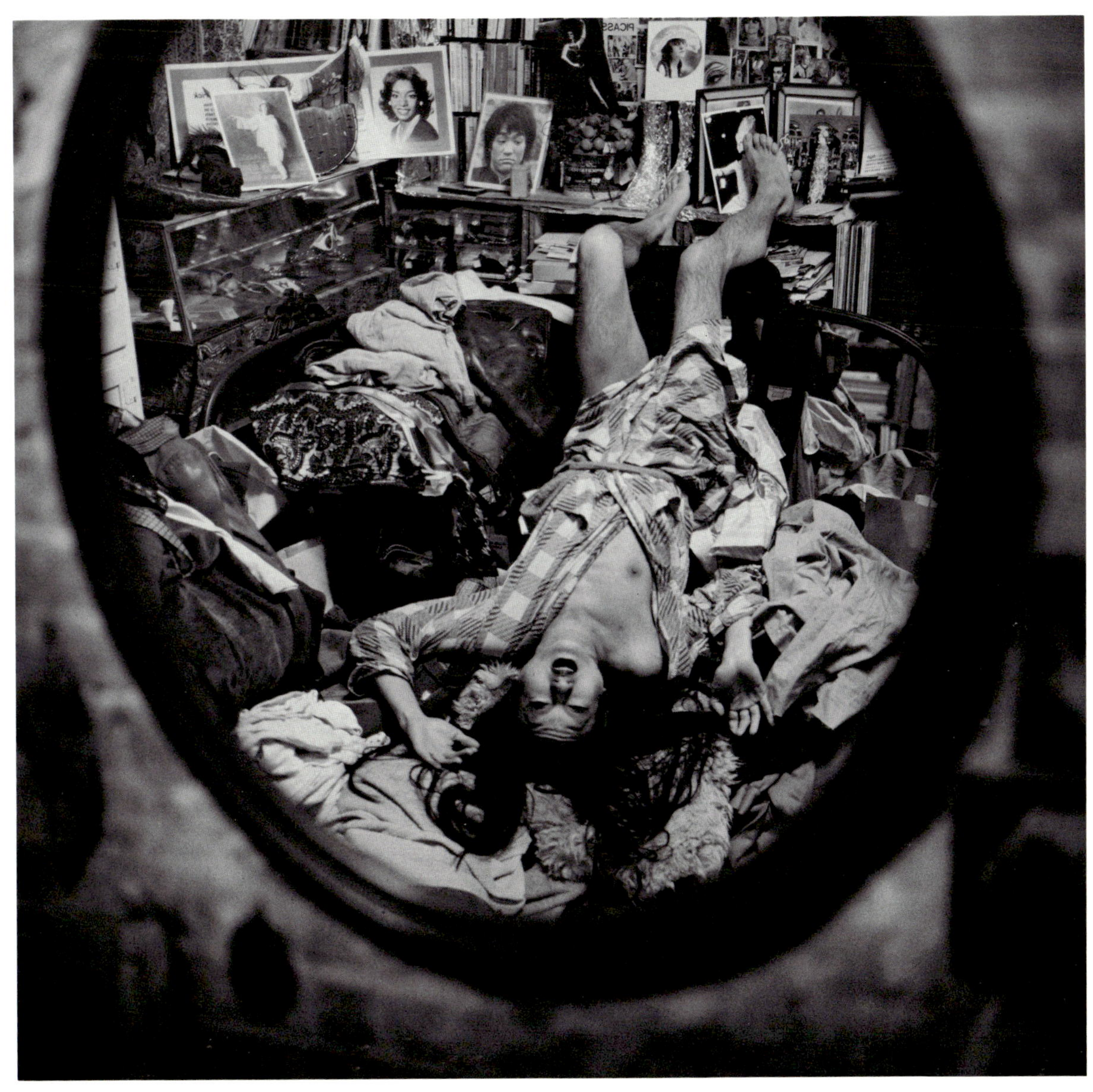

Girl in Attic, Rhinebeck, New York

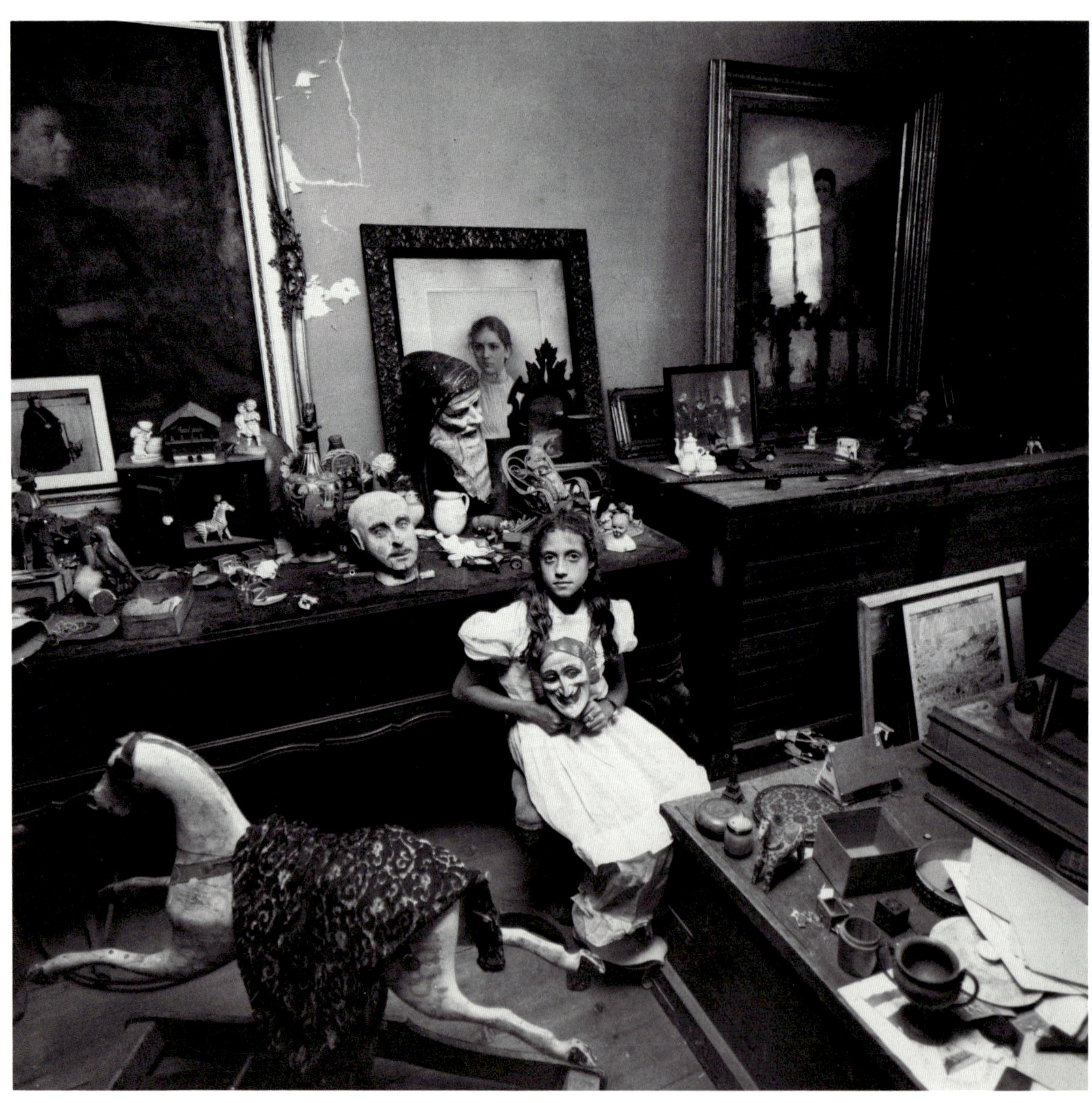

L. B. Broadmore, Piano tuner, Tivoli, New York

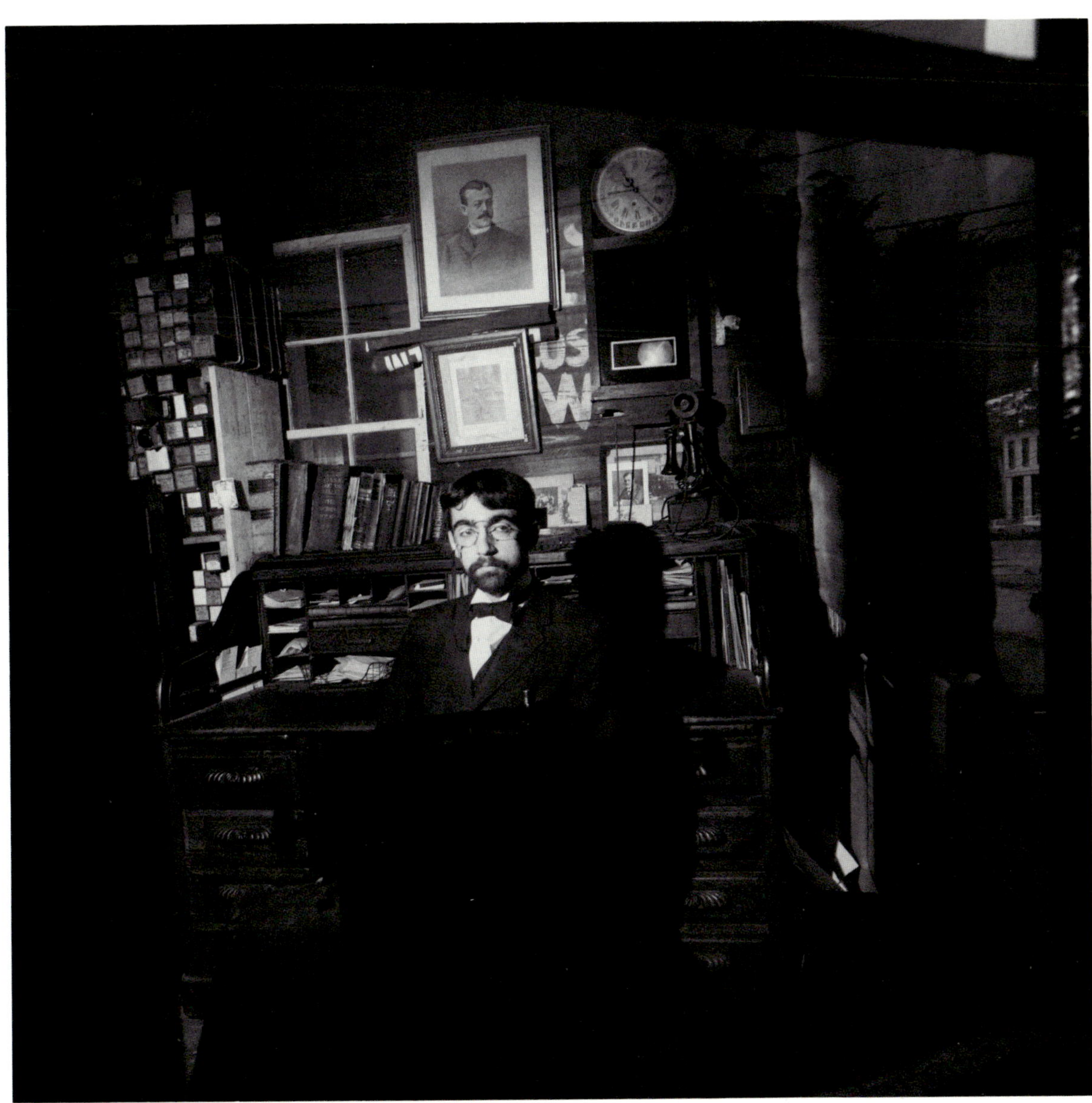

Carol Blanchard, Painter, New York City

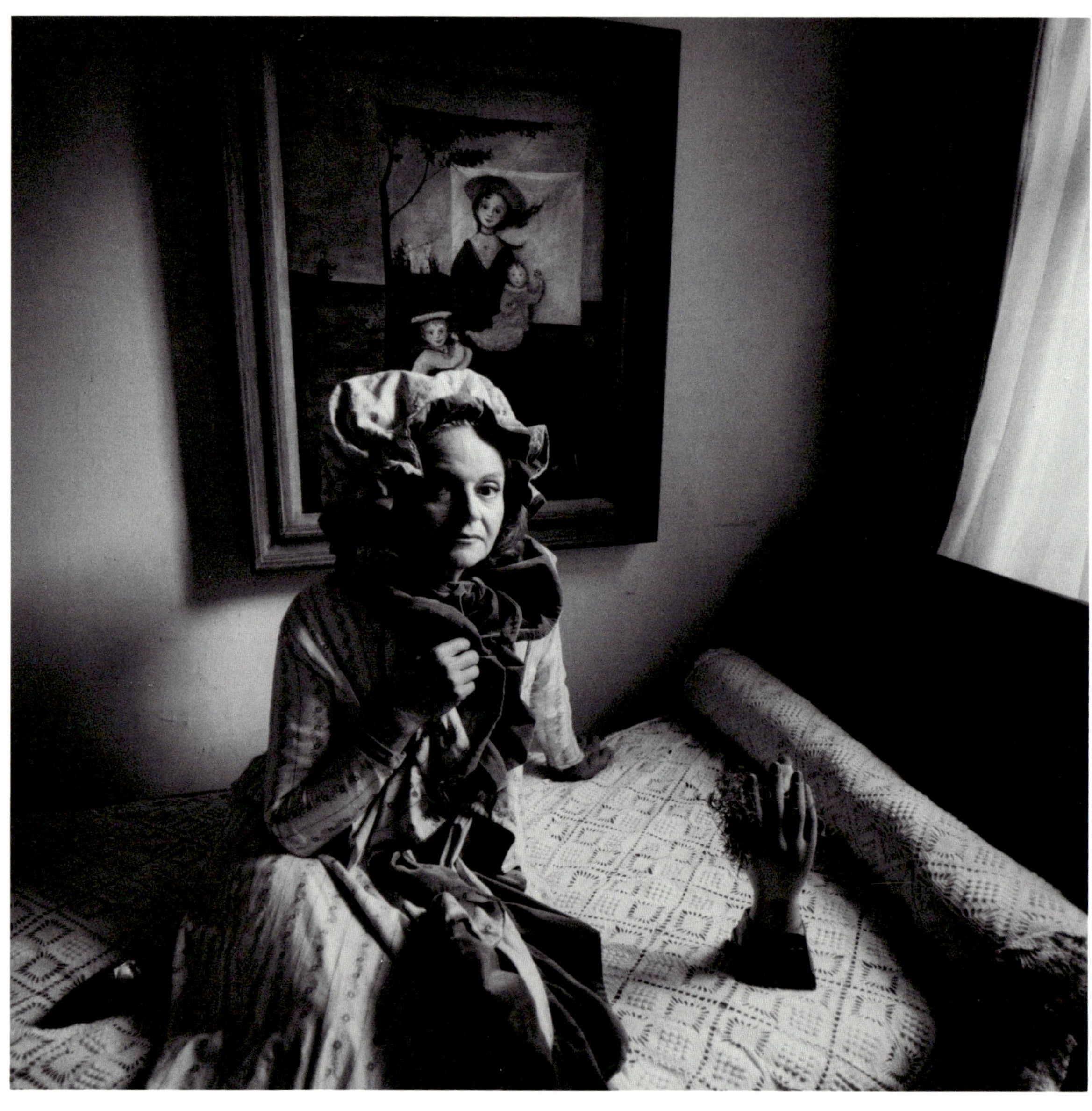

Peg Littlefield, Dolls, Martha's Vineyard

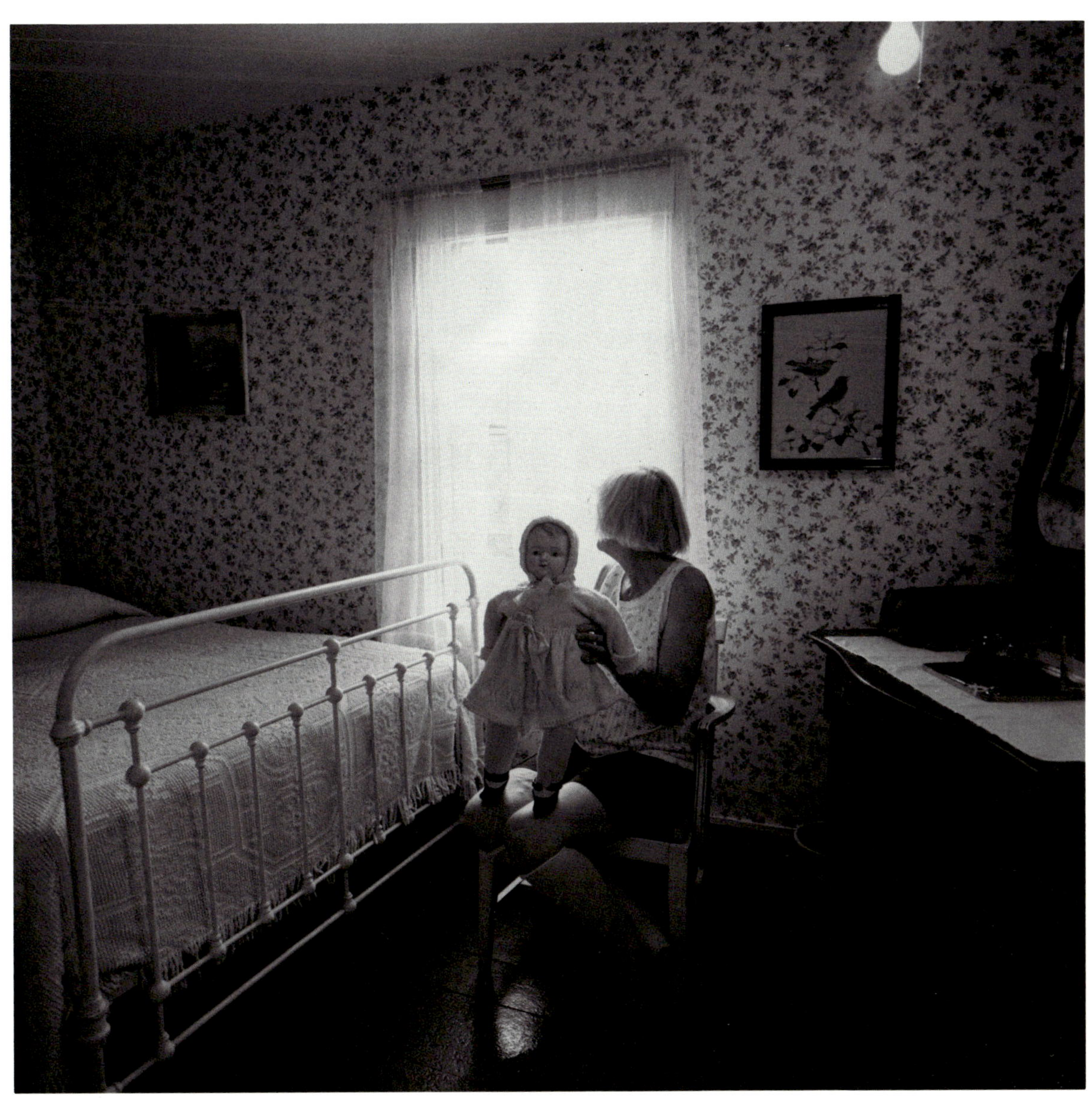

DIRECTORS OF DARKNESS

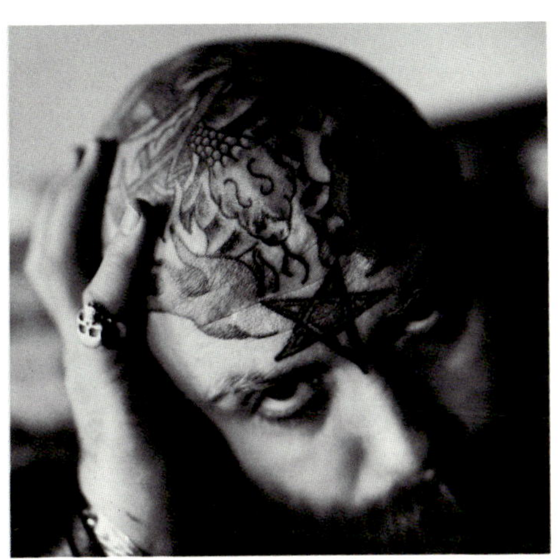

Robin Lanz, Magician, New York City

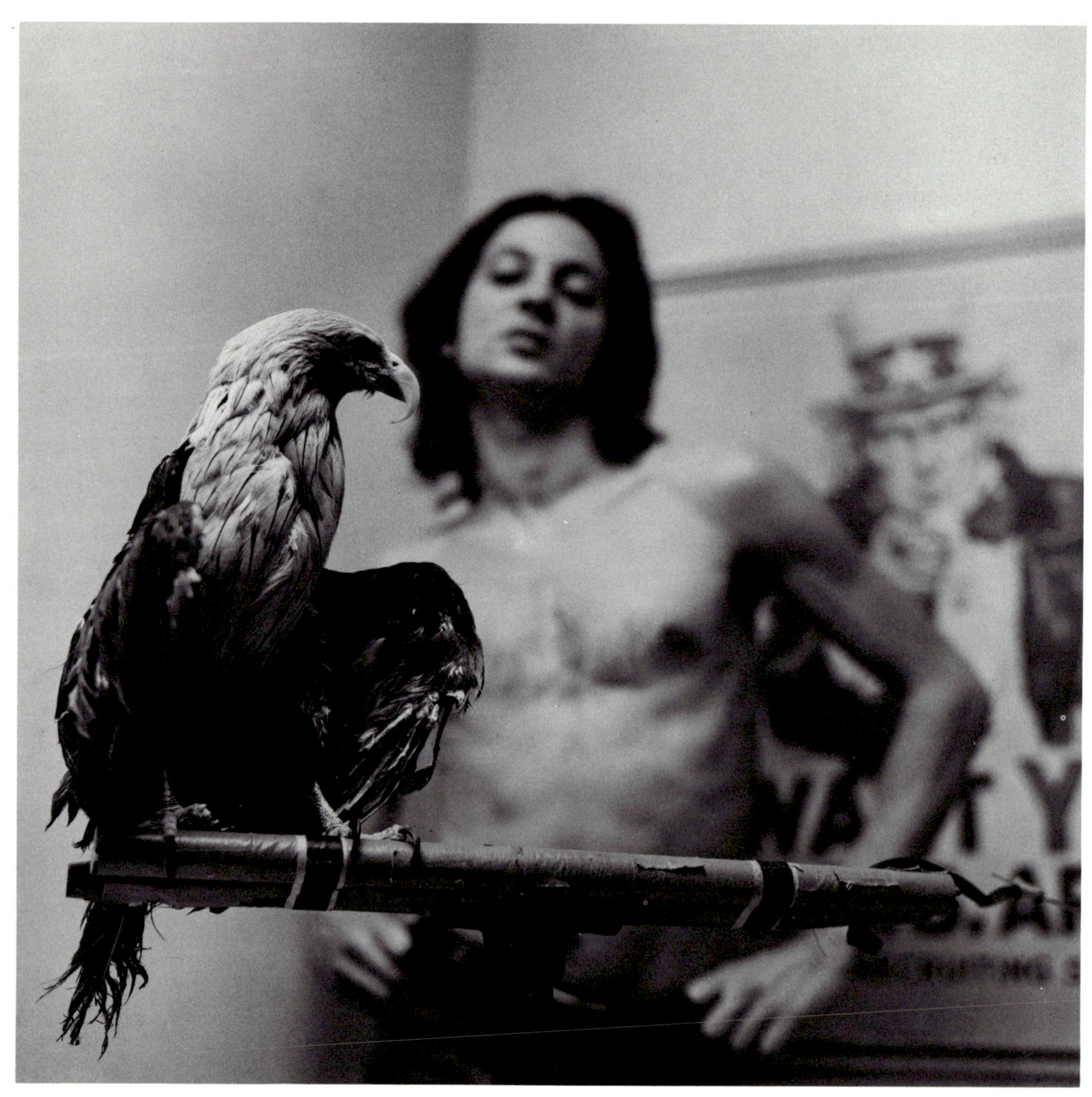

Charles Ludlum, Punchman, New York City

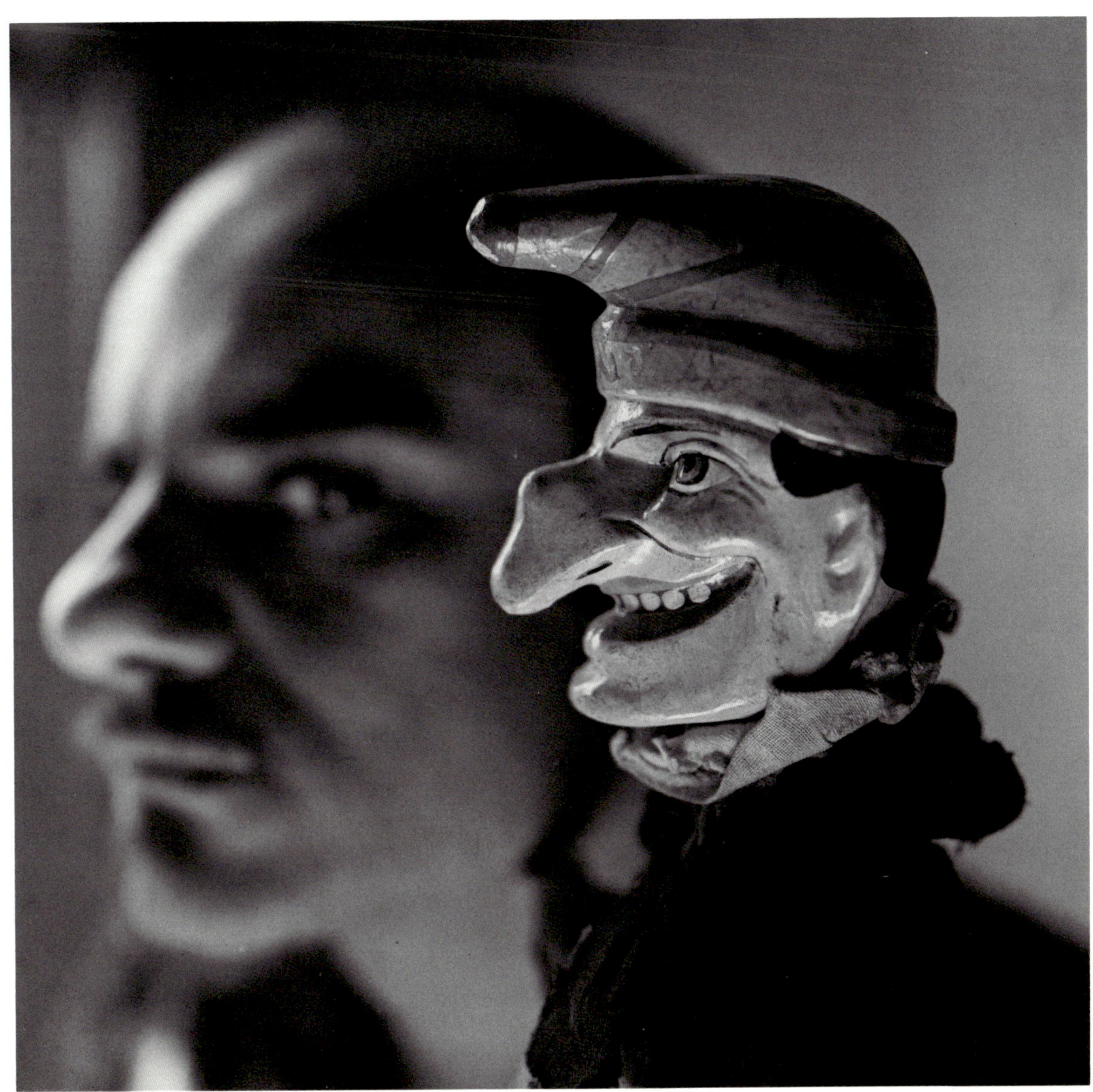

Alain Blair, Trainer, New York City

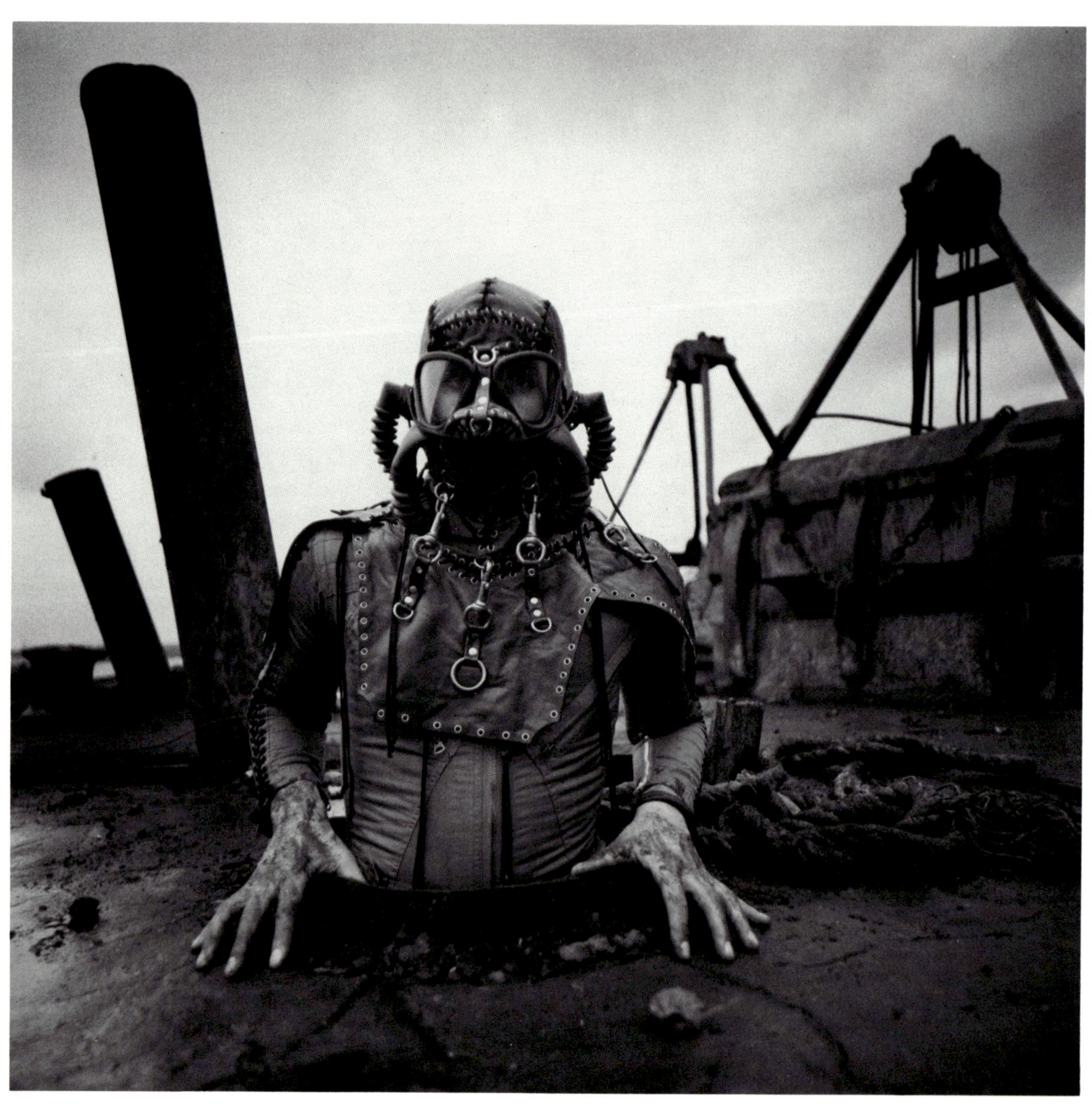

Reginald Thyer, Wizard, Montour Falls, New York

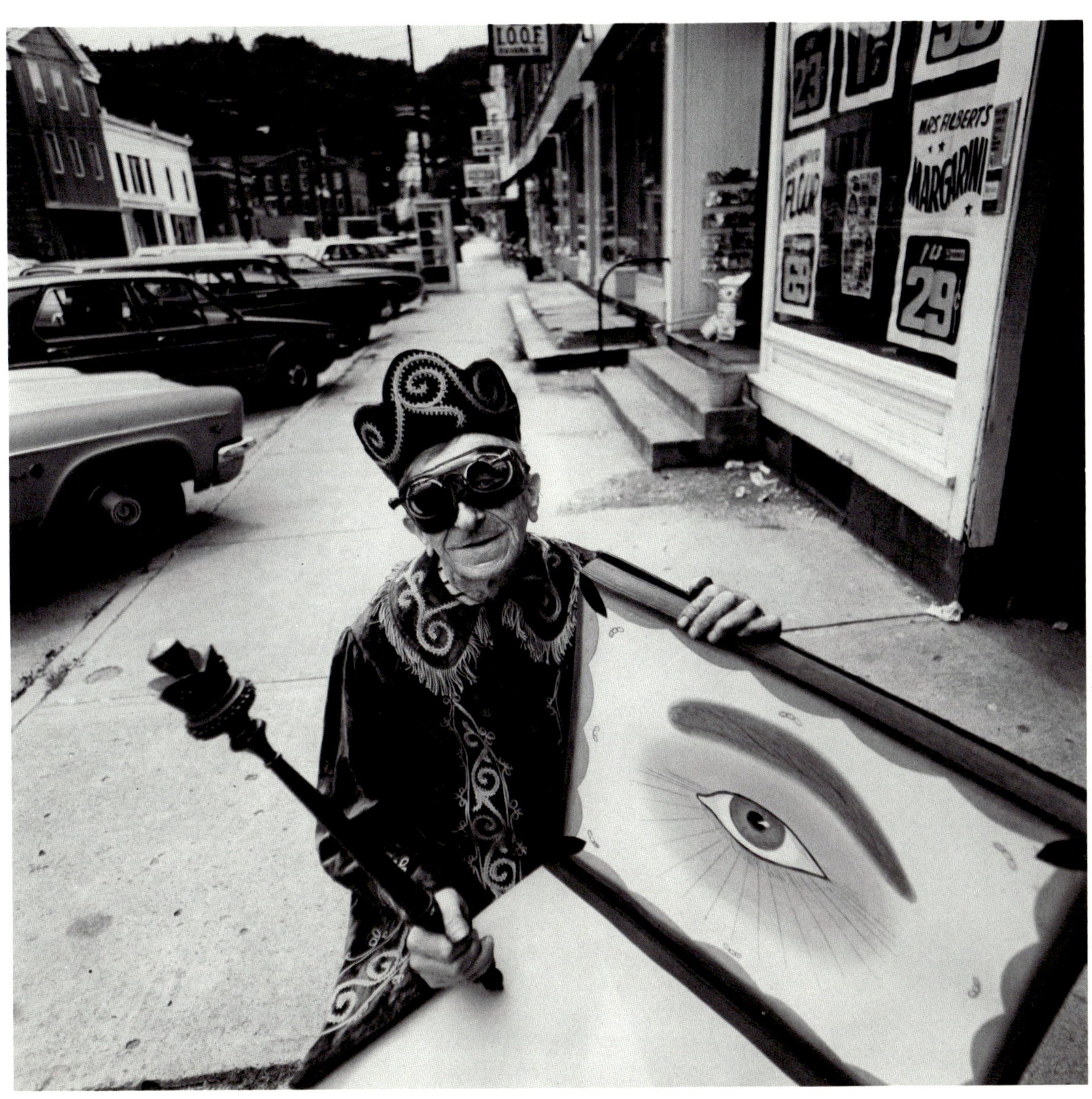

Minette, Chanteuse, New York City

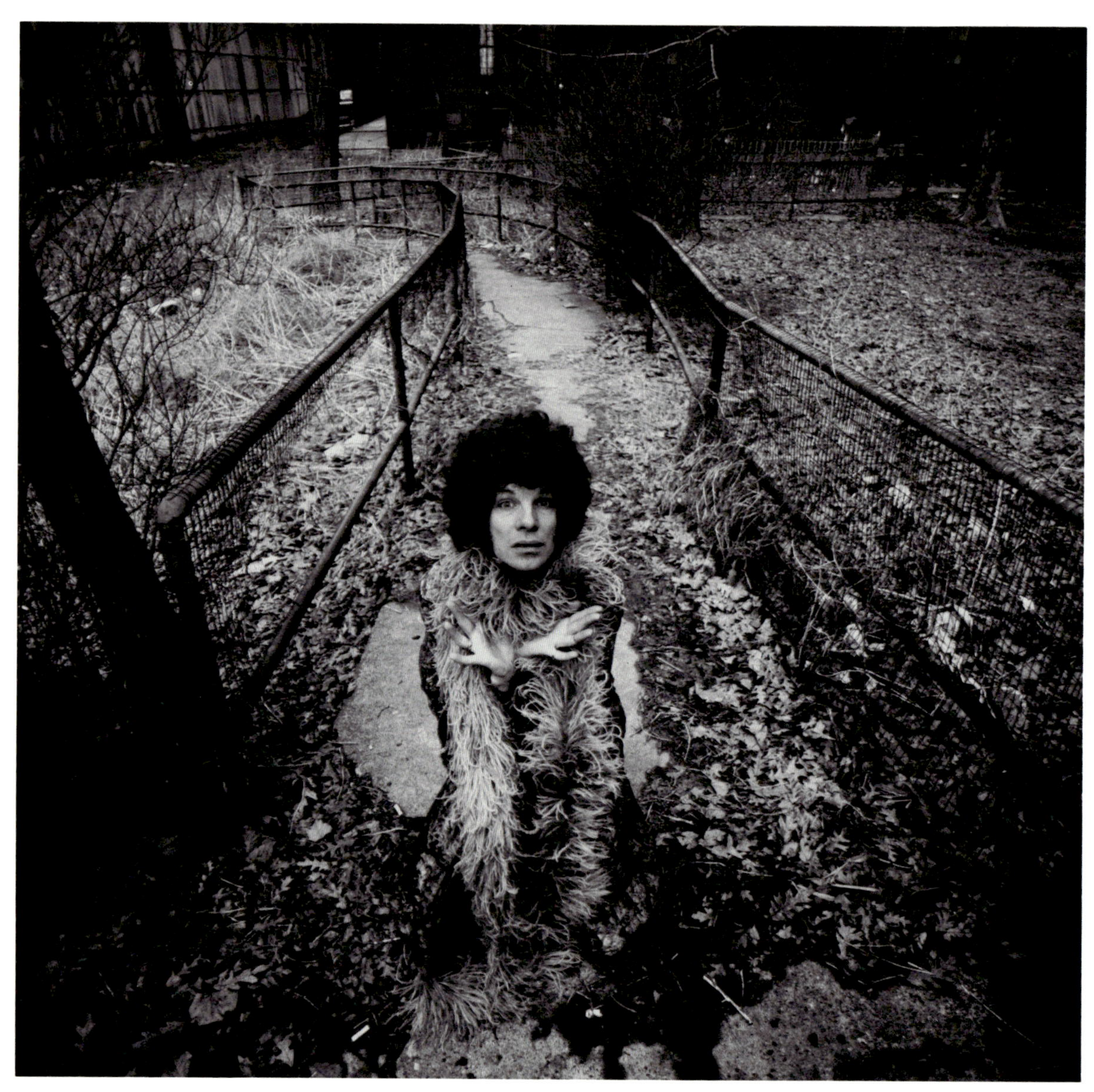

Stephan Brecht, Actor, New York City

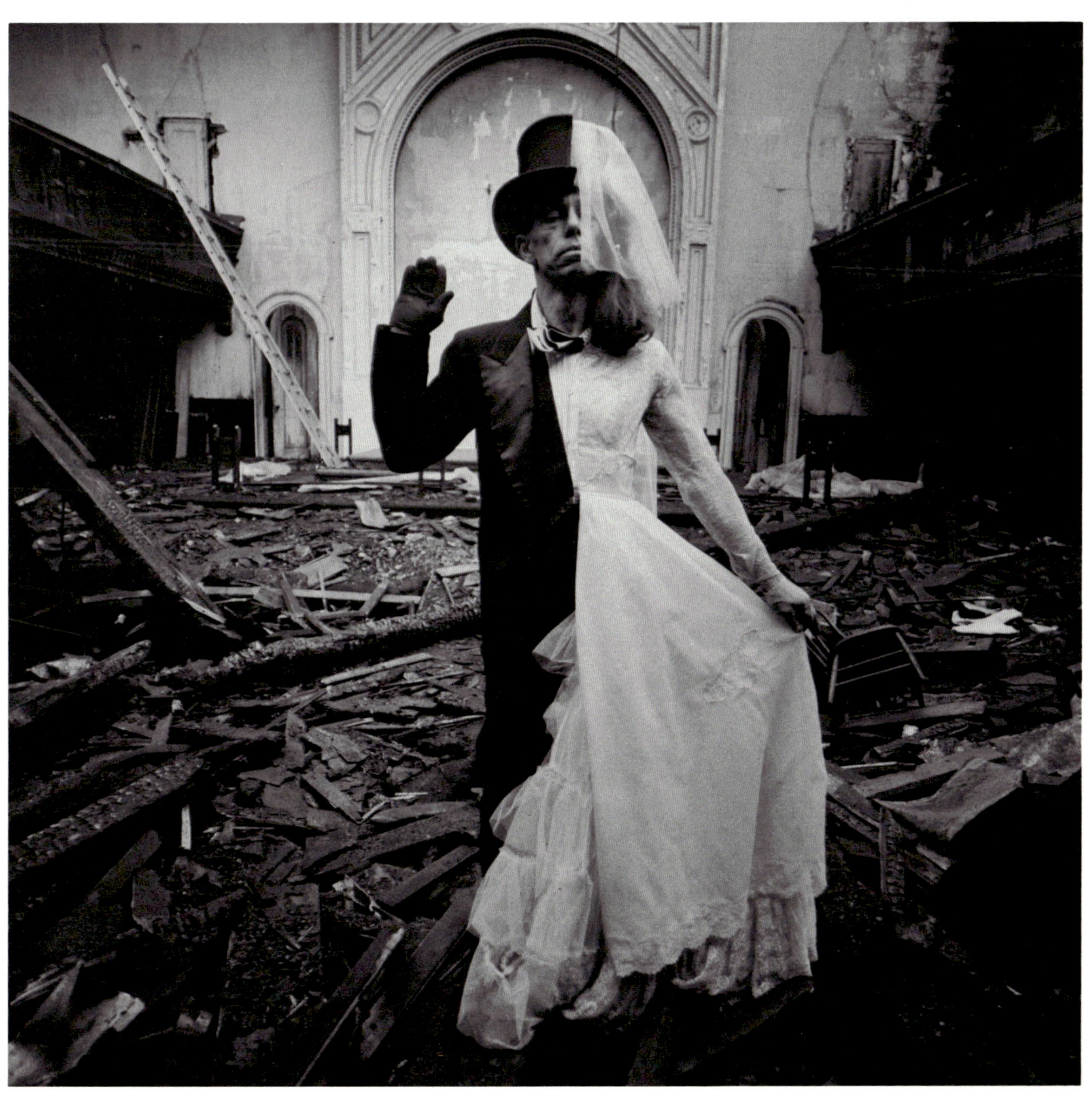

Betty Bersch, Clairvoyant, New York City

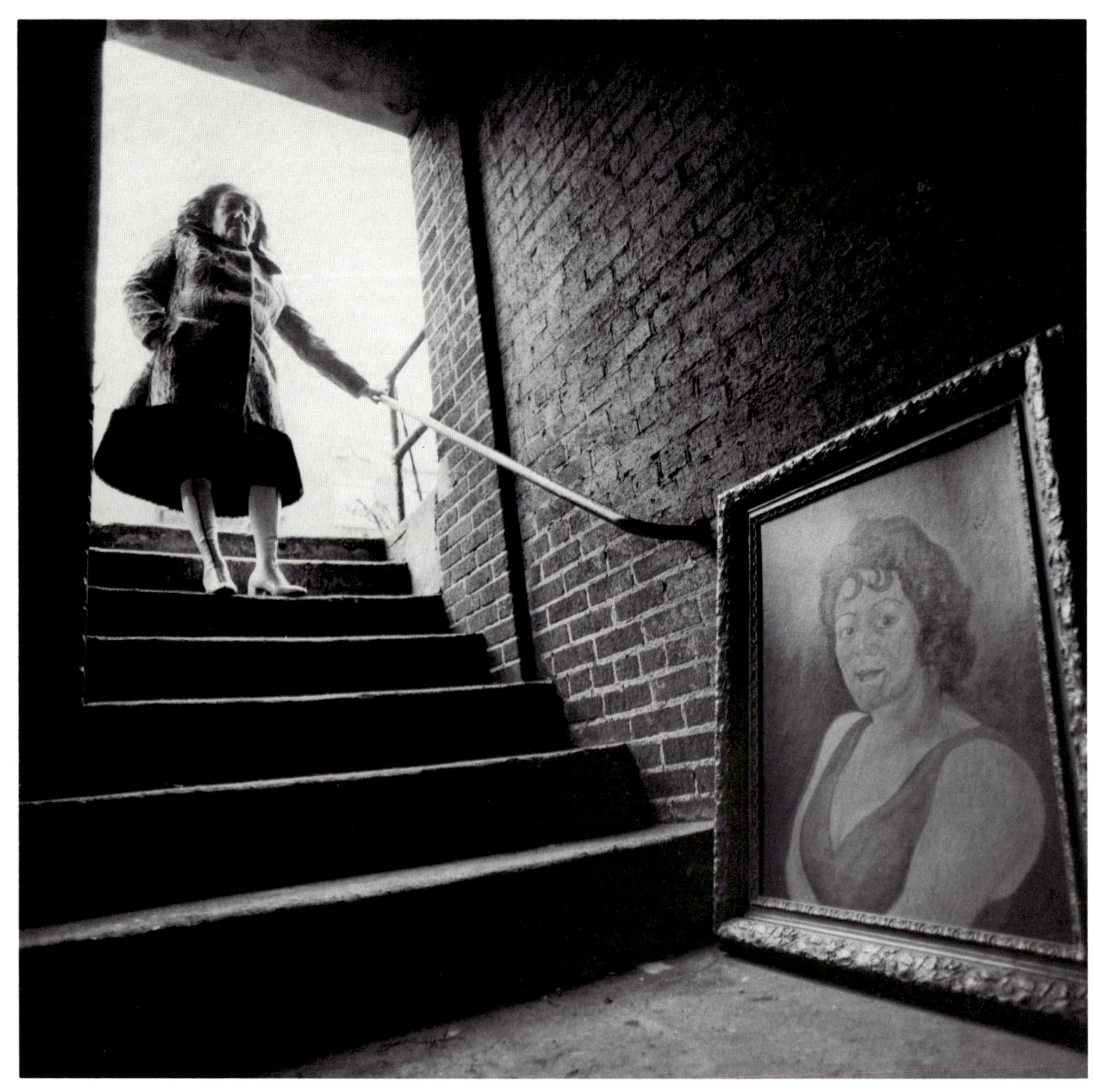

Harold Ellis, Dream Therapist, New York City

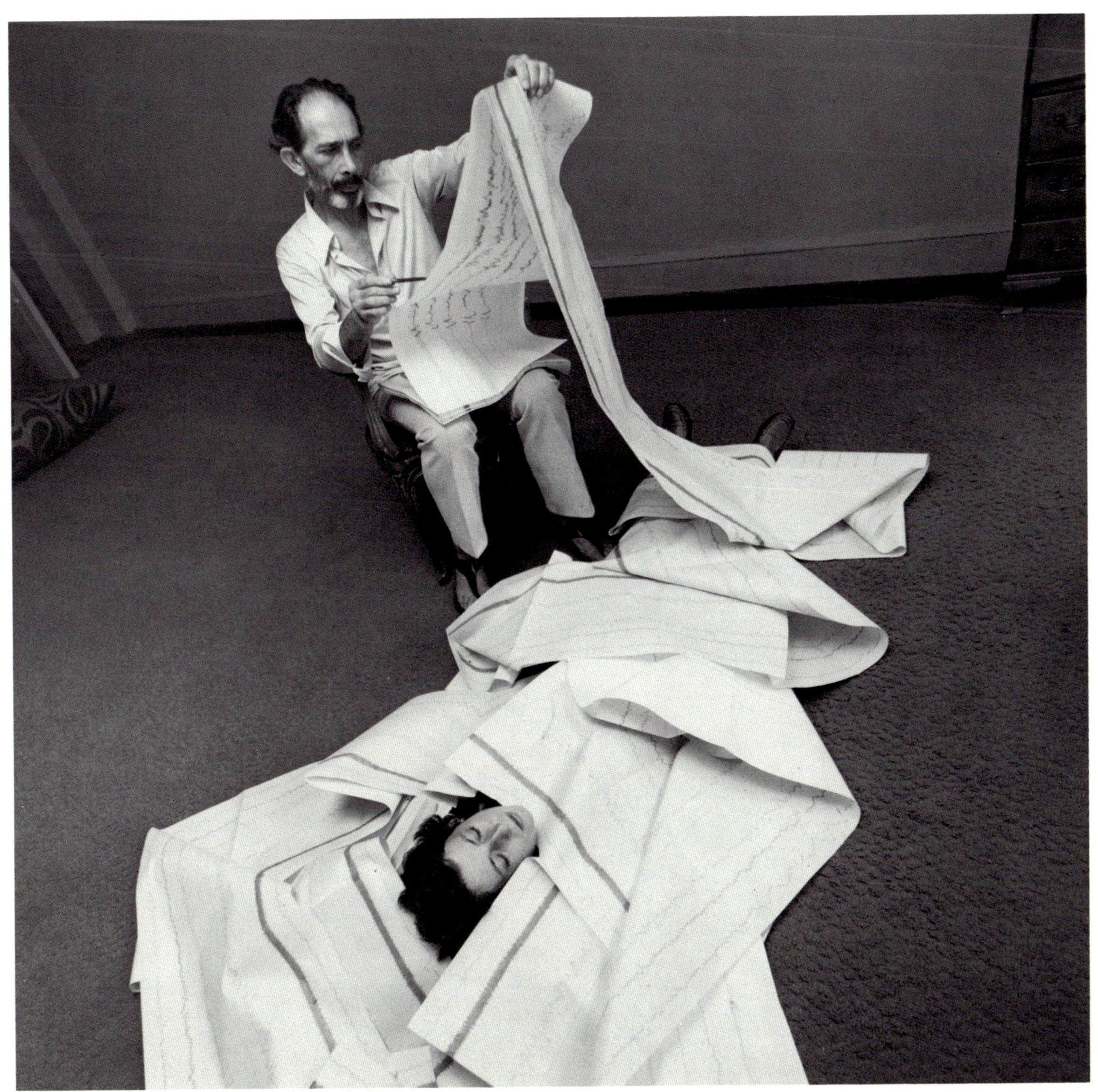

FINAL CURTAIN

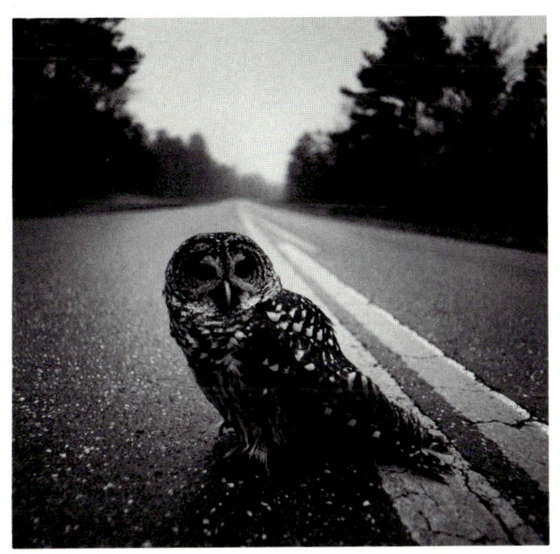

Computer Programmer, Berkeley, California

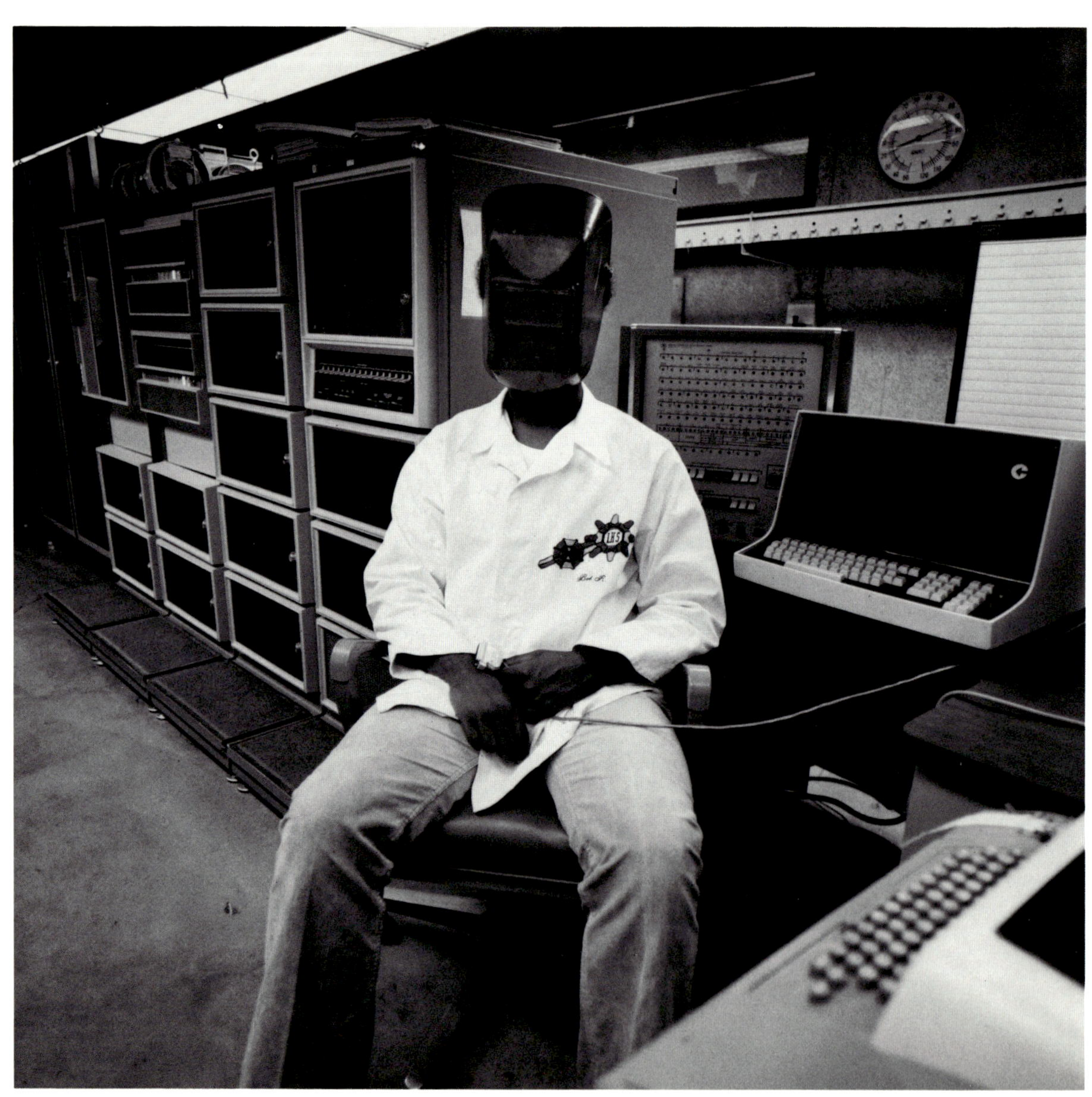

Space Program Scientist, Washington, D.C.

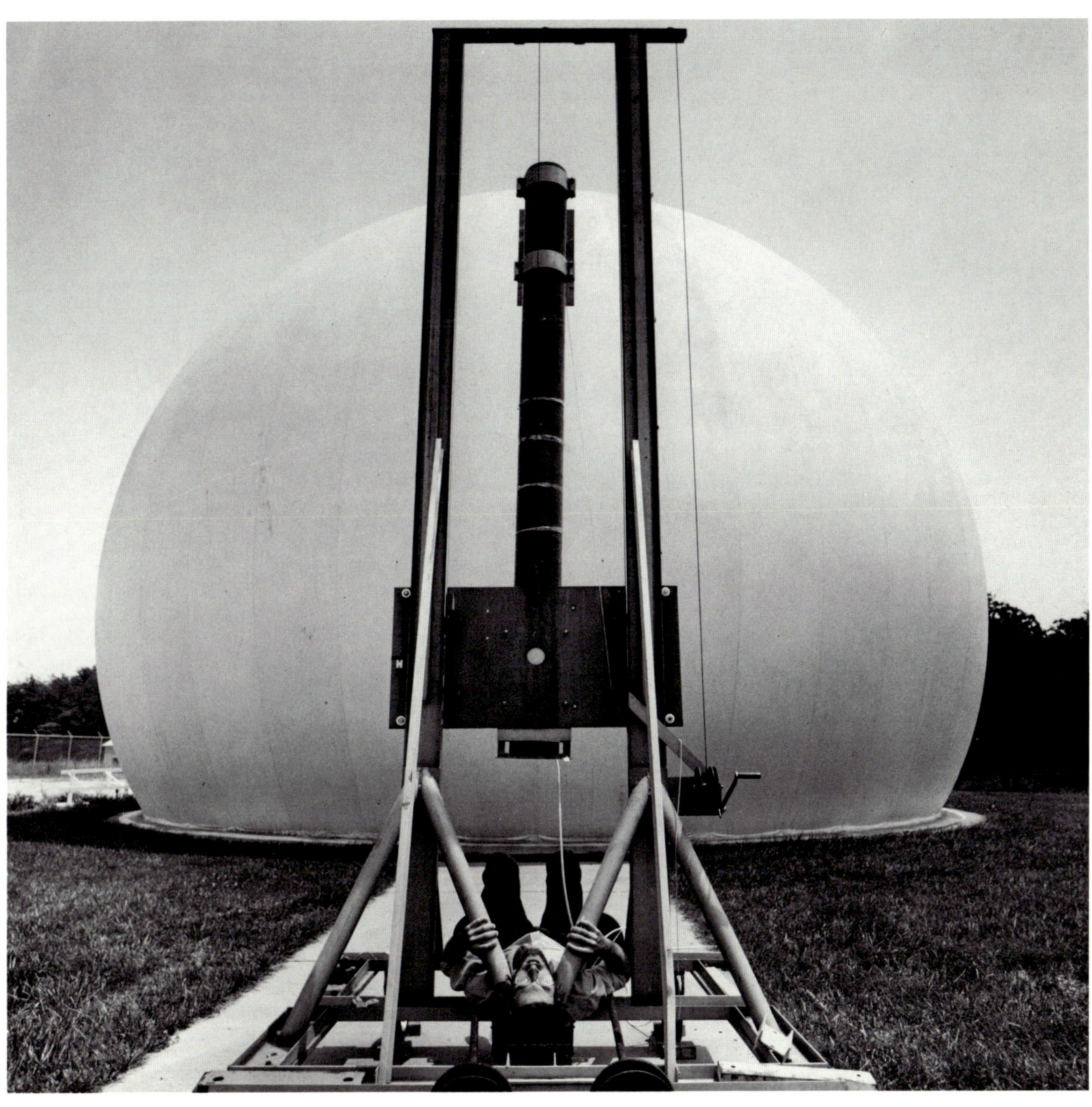

Unisex Styling School, New York City

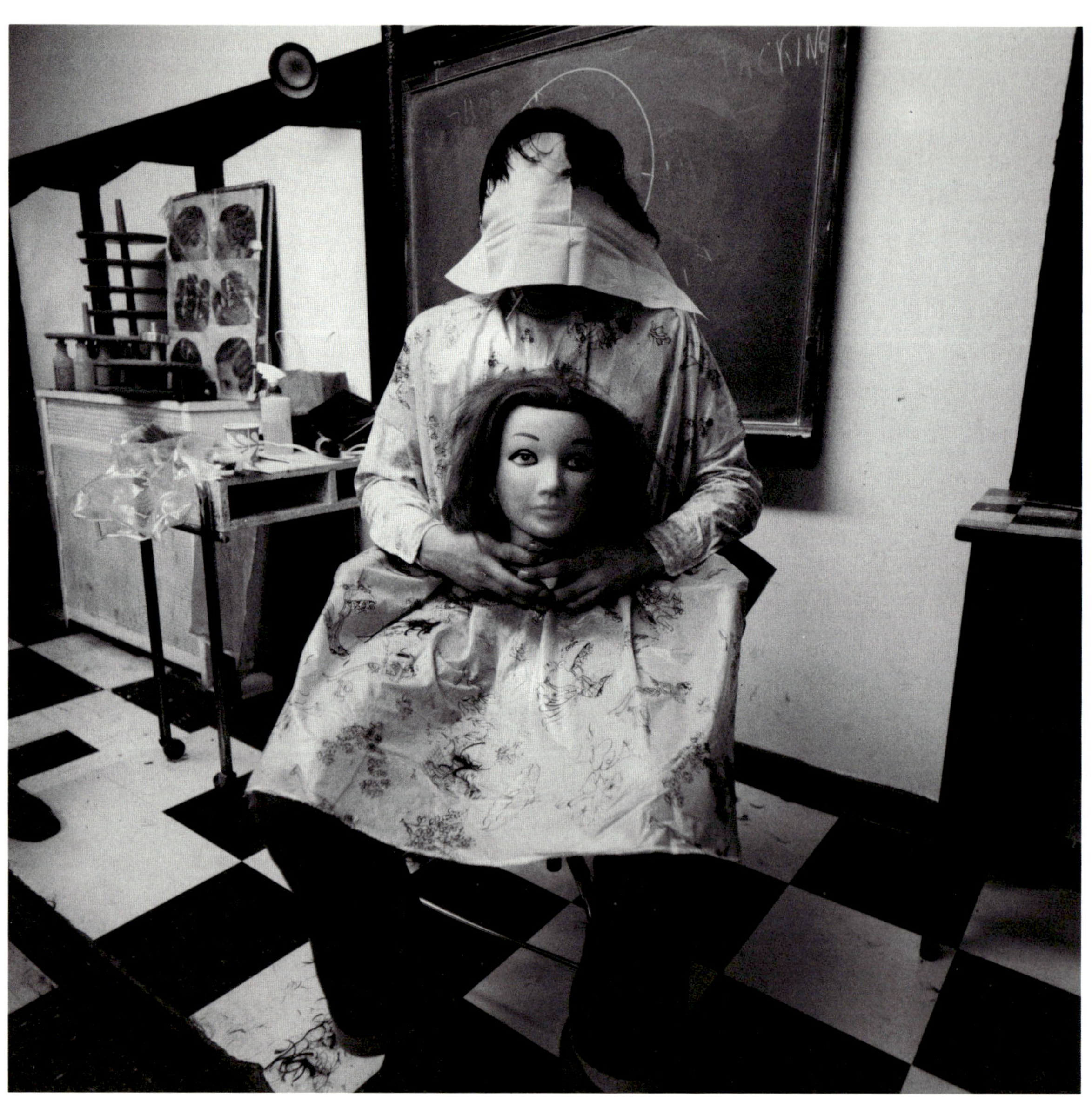

Medical Student with deformed Baby Doll, New York City

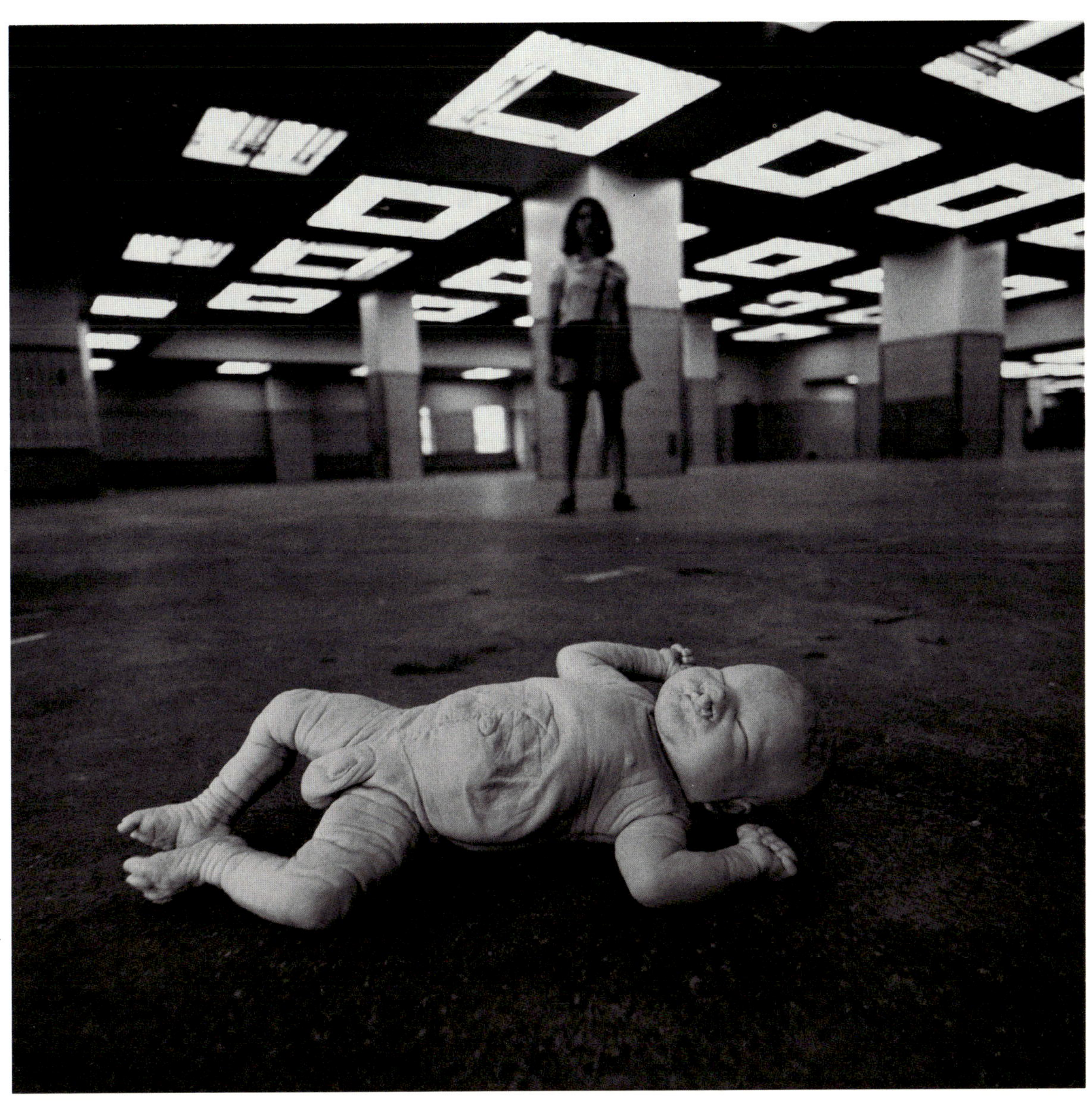

Nurse with Boy, Children's Ward, New York City

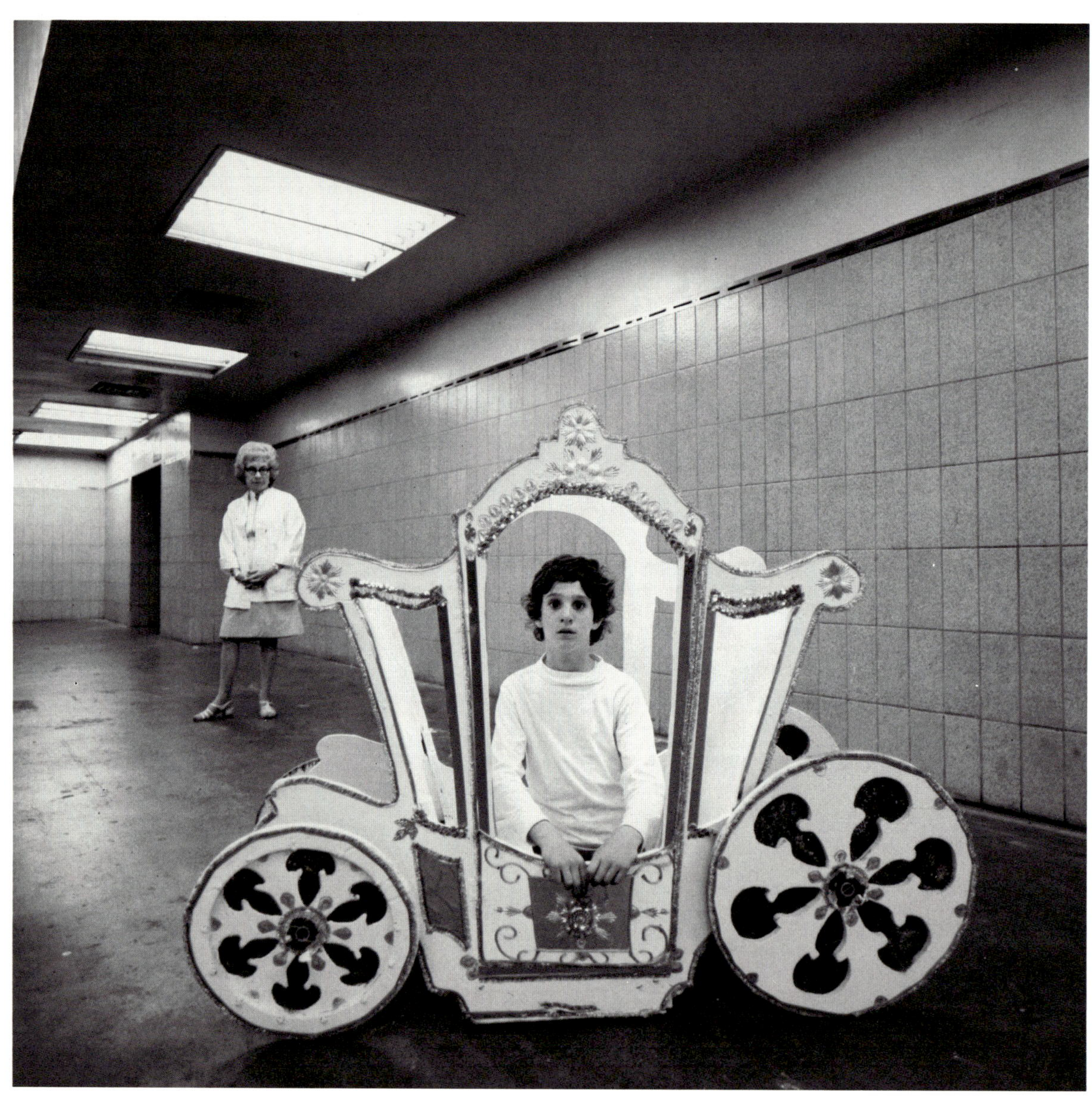

Doctor and Patient, Bellevue, New York City

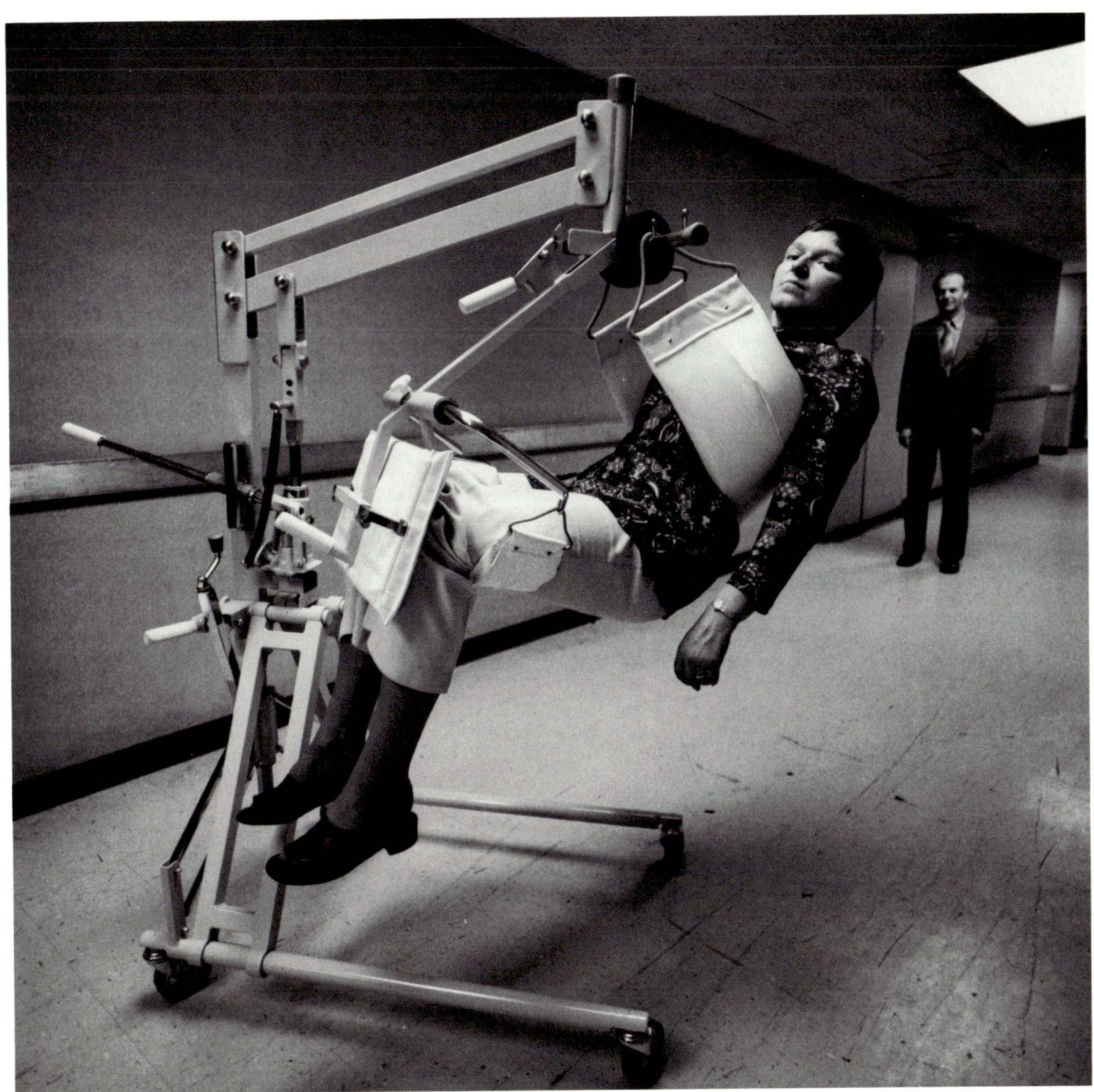

Doctor and Bones, Cape May, New Jersey

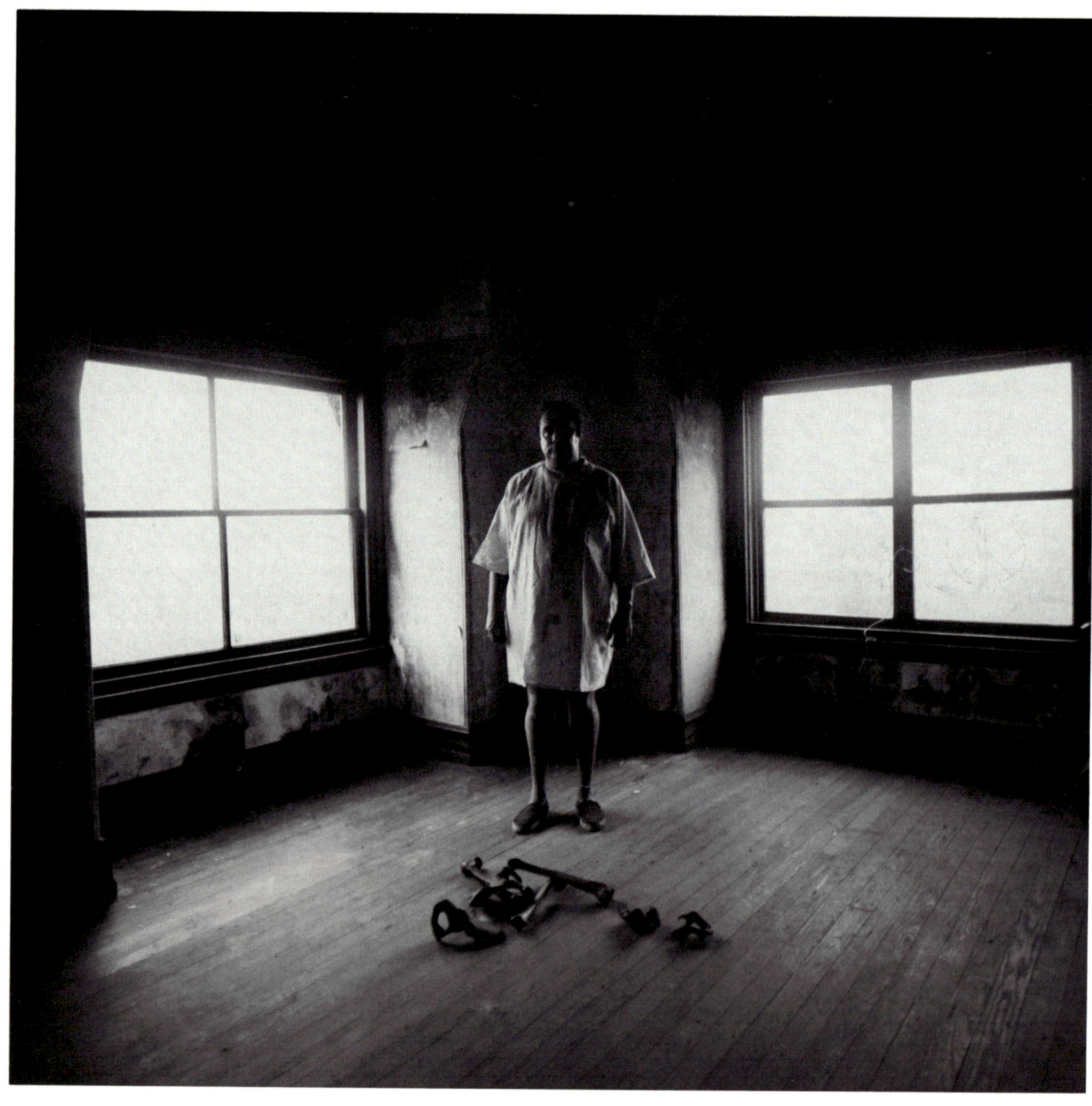

Operating Table, Osteopathic Hospital, New York City

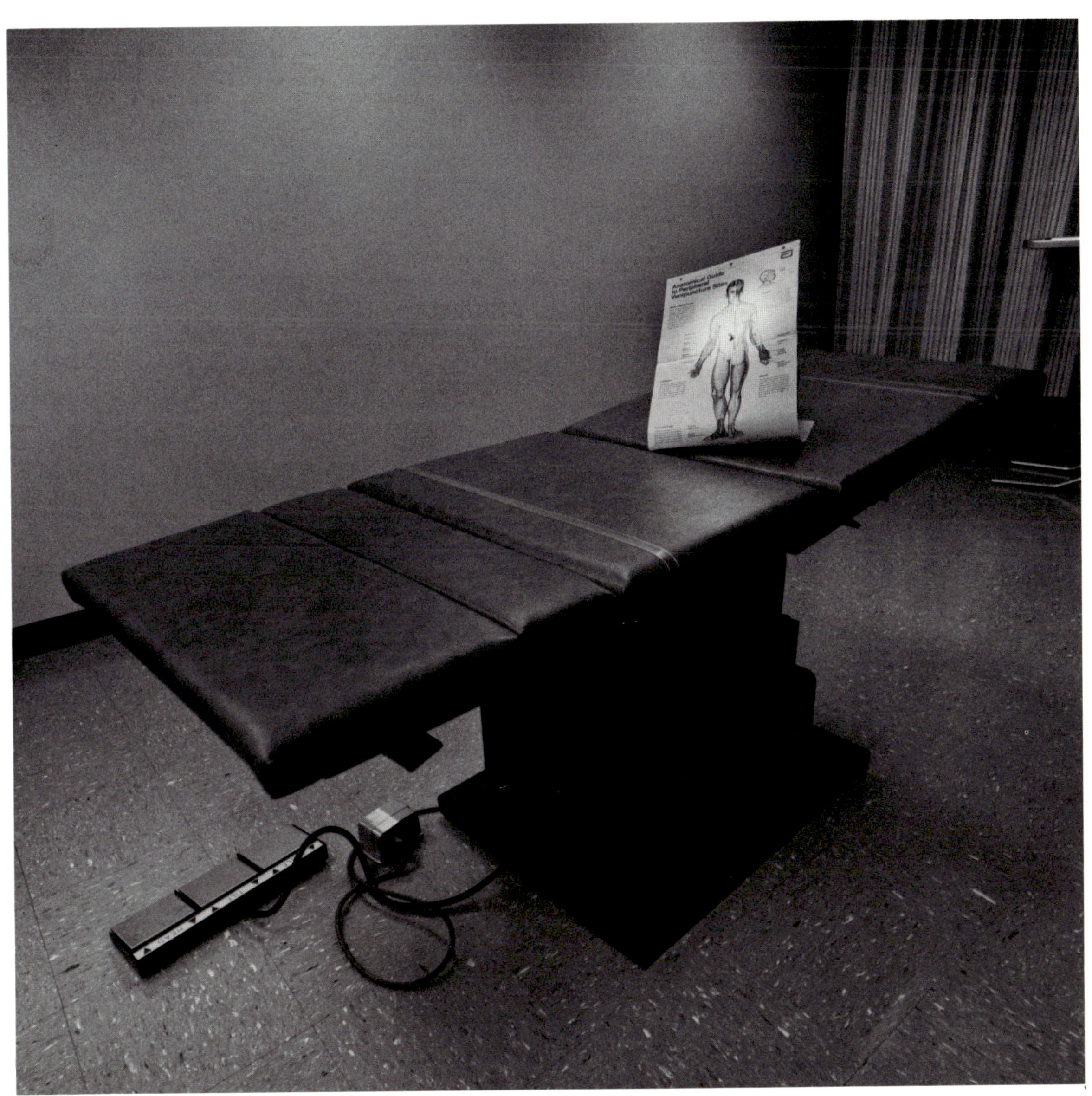

Woman enacting Death Dream, White Plains Cemetery, New York

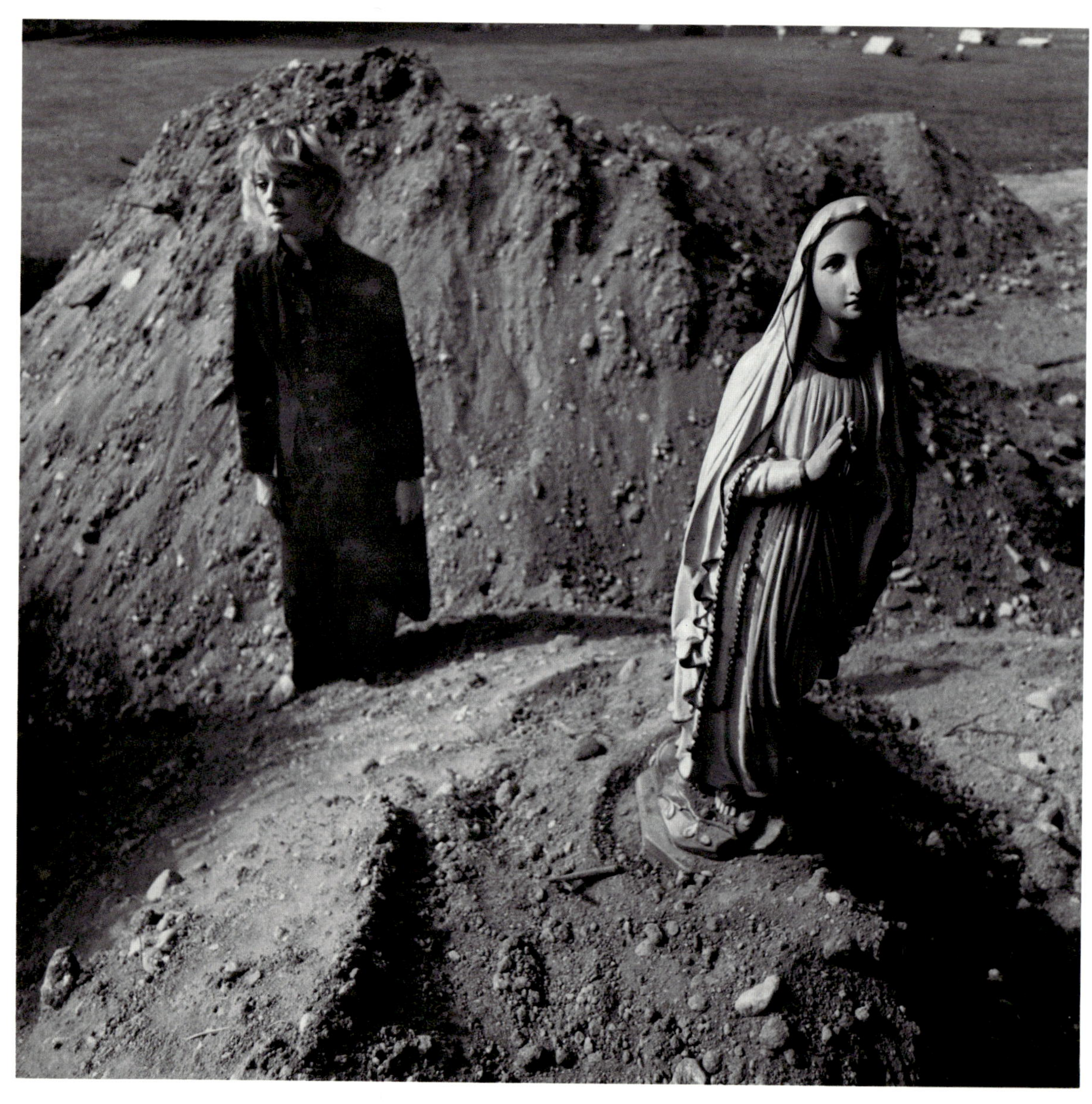

Woman on Roof, New York City

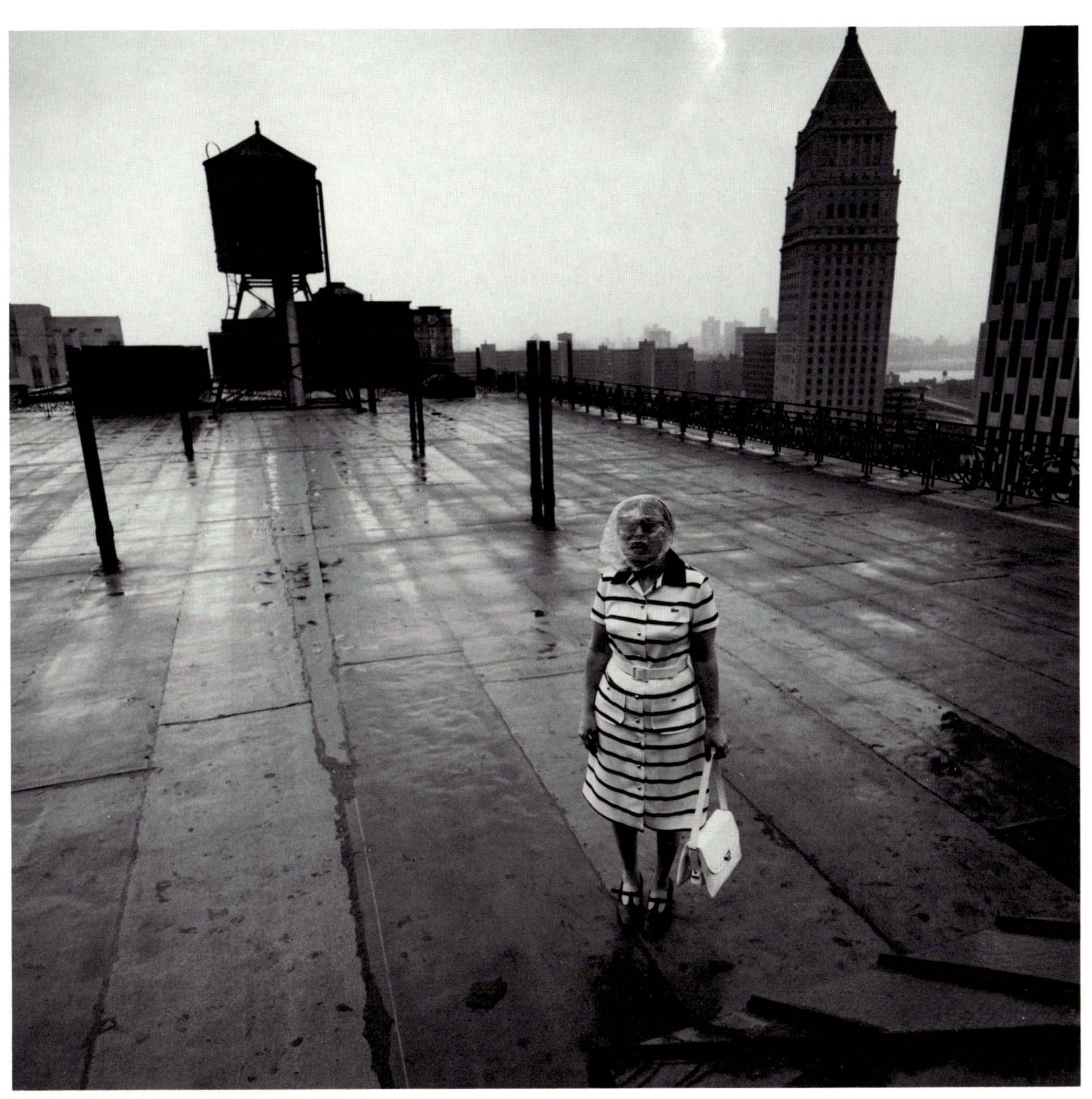

Philip Hecksher's Dream, Bar Harbor, Maine

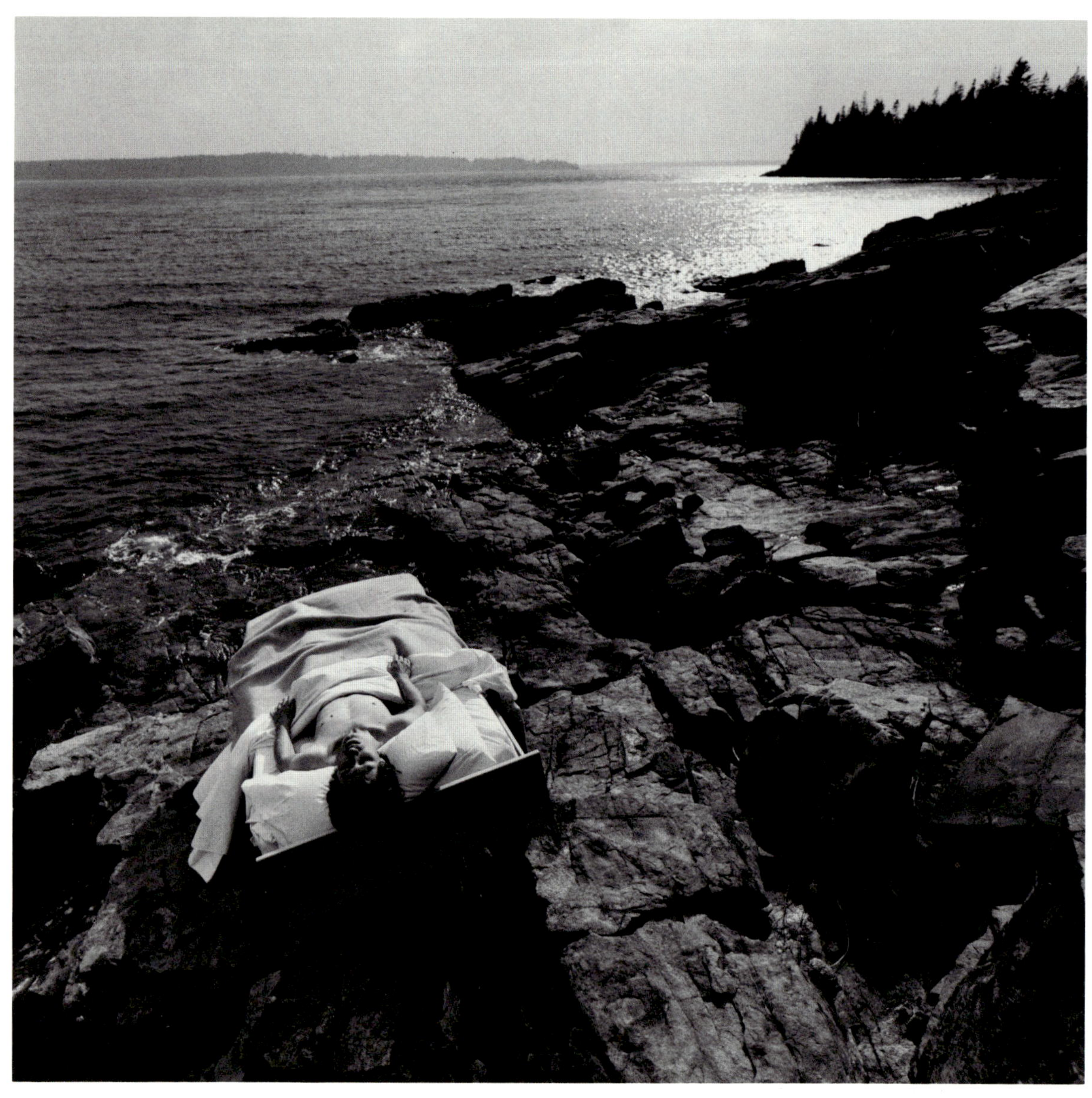

Claire de Lune, Breezy Point, New York

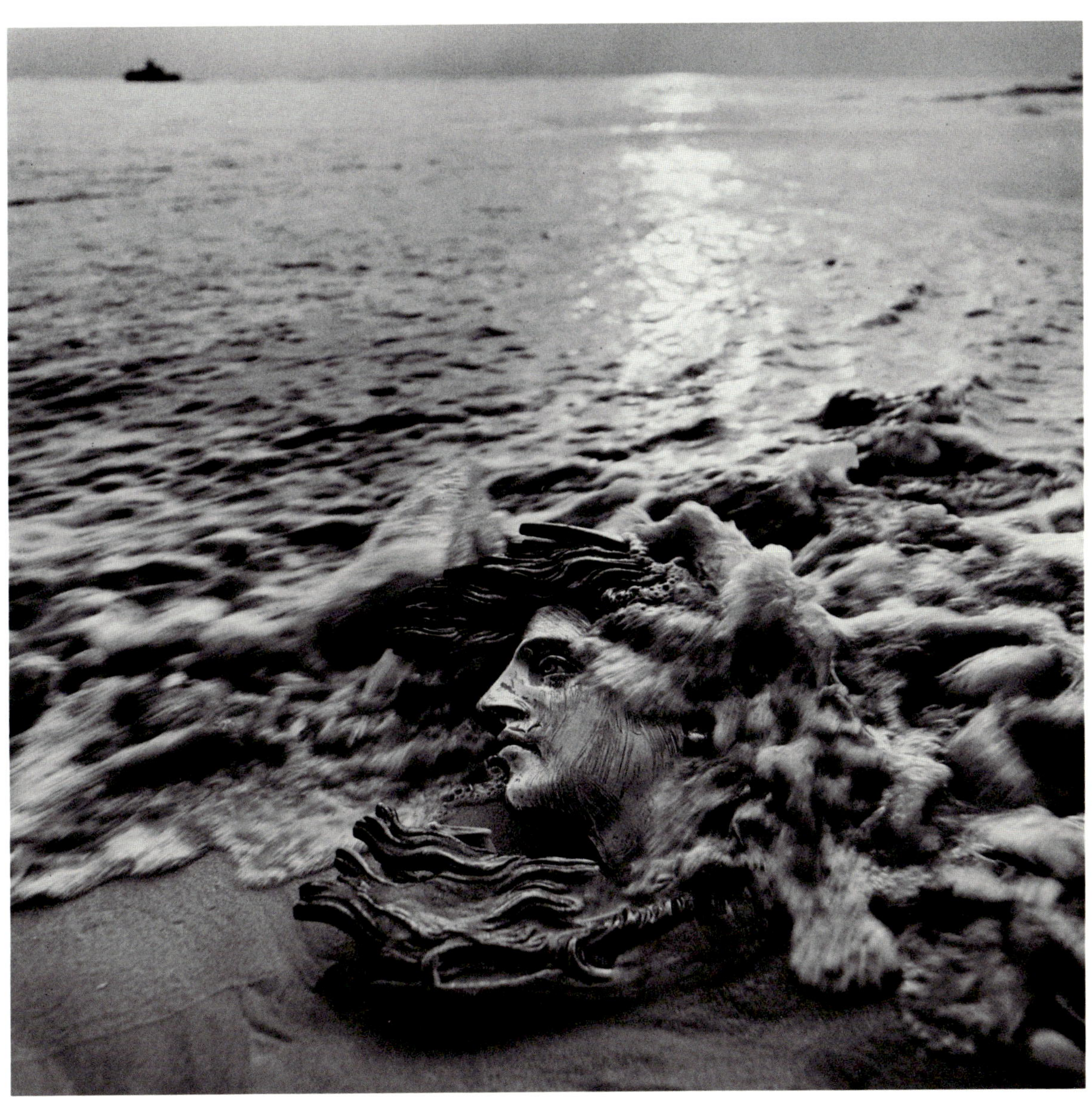